MORSE CODE WRENS
OF STATION X

Bletchley's Outer Circle

Anne Glyn-Jones
Petty Officer Telegraphist,
WRNS, 1942–1945

AMPHORA
PRESS

amphorapress.com

Amphora Press is the trade books division
of Imprint Academic Ltd.

Published in the UK by
Imprint Academic Ltd., PO Box 200, Exeter EX5 5YX, UK

Distributed in the USA by
Ingram Book Company,
One Ingram Blvd., La Vergne, TN 37086, USA

ISBN 9781845409081 paperback
ISBN 9781845409098 hardback

A CIP catalogue record for this book is available from the
British Library and US Library of Congress

Cover image courtesy of the Imperial War Museum,
used with permission.

Contents

HRH The Princess Royal

Foreword

BUCKINGHAM PALACE

In 2017 we celebrate the 100th anniversary of the founding of the Women's Royal Naval Service (WRNS). During the First World War the Royal Navy became the first of the three services to recruit women. Nicknamed 'Wrens' the women were initially recruited to release men to serve at sea, but as the Navy expanded so did the Wrens' responsibilities to include driving, operating radar equipment, planning naval operations, and code breaking work.

Intercepting German Morse Code signals was one of the jobs Wrens were tasked with when recruited to 'Station X', or Bletchley Park, and its outstations known as 'Y Stations'. We now know just how important this undercover work was, and the Wrens played a vital part making up around 75% of the workforce.

The WRNS was integrated into the Royal Navy in 1993 but still has approximately 45,000 former members ranging in age from their thirties to their nineties. As patron of the WRNS Benevolent Trust I am delighted that Anne Glyn-Jones, now aged 94, has been able to leave us this valuable contribution to the WRNS' history. Her bravery, tenacity and discretion are a shining example to younger women today wanting to make a contribution to society by serving those around them.

Prologue

Since the commitment to secrecy, to which we were all bound, began to be relaxed in the late 1970s, much has been said and written about the contribution to the war effort of the code-breakers of Bletchley Park. Much less has been made known about the lives and work of those without whom Bletchley Park would have had no texts on which to work, the men and women of all three Services and even beyond who became what Sinclair Mackay called, in his pioneering work of 2012, *The Secret Listeners*, or, as it was called (from WI, Wireless Intelligence), the Y-Branch. Some were linguists, listening to spoken enemy radio transmissions; others were telegraphists, trained in Morse communications. This memoir seeks to expand their story so far as one group was concerned — the WRNS contingent of telegraphists.

There were listening stations all over the world, facilitated by the widespread reach of the British Empire. Security ensured that those who worked at them had no idea either of the existence of Bletchley Park or of our relationship to it. I once overheard a charge-hand (they were civilian operators, who had gone into pre-war Y work on retirement from the Royal Navy) say, in relation to a problem at work, "Maybe BP could help us with that one", and I presumed they were not referring to Buckingham Palace, but I did not ask, and would have been reprimanded if I had. 'Need to know' was always the criterion, and I did not need to know. Marion Hill's *Bletchley Park People*, published in 2004, pinpoints the mindset we were required to develop. At Bletchley a 1942 security warning emphasized the importance of discretion even within Bletchley itself. "Do not talk at meals. Do not talk in the transport. Do not talk travelling. Do not talk in the billet. Do not talk by your own fireside. Be careful even in your hut."

We heard only of 'Station X', where we presumed someone was trying, though with what degree of success we did not know, to decode the messages we so diligently transcribed. Despatch riders took away the messages we wrote down, but no one knew to what destination they rode. Transmission was later bolstered by teleprinters, and Wren teleprinter operators appeared on the scene. How messages reached Station X from overseas listening posts we had no idea.

The first crack in the security wall appeared in 1974, with the publication of F.W. Winterbotham's *The Ultra Secret*, and only then, more than thirty years after I got involved, did I first learn of the existence of 'Bletchley Park'. During the 1970s, records containing Enigma/Ultra material began to be released to the Public Record Office, and this led to enquiries as to whether we were still subject to our vows of secrecy — vows which were life-long, not governed by the so-called 'thirty years rule'. David Owen MP, then Foreign Secretary, made clear in a written answer to a question in the House of Commons in January 1978 that while it was permissible for those involved to say what they had been doing during the war, any reference to the content of their work must not go beyond what had been released to the PRO, and any information as to how the information had been obtained remained classified.

In 1979 came the first volume of F.H. Hinsley's magisterial official history, *British Intelligence in the Second World War,* Vol. II of which, published in 1981, covered the story of Bletchley's involvement in the U-boat battles in which the Wren telegraphists were so deeply engaged. Following these revelations, a leading British military historian, commissioned by Oxford University Press to write a definitive history of the Y-Branch, contacted some of us for help, and we asked the then Foreign Secretary, Geoffrey Howe, where we stood. Though by now a trickle of books was beginning to appear, and presumably receiving clearance, we were referred back to David Owen's restrictive guidance of 1978. The historian sadly died in 1984, so that ended the possibility of seeing our story told.

Throughout the 1980s the Bletchley site remained neglected, the huts sinking into dereliction and the site attracting development interest for housing. In May 1991 the Bletchley Archaeological and Historical Society formed a committee to trace Bletchley veterans for a Farewell Party designed to put final closure to Bletchley's wartime story. Over 100 people came, and their reminiscences led to the determination to save the site as a memorial to the work that had been done there. In February 1992 the Bletchley Park Trust was formed, and by arrangement with the landlords, the site was opened to visitors in 1994. Anxious negotiations and fund-raising over the next five years led to the site being permanently secured in June 1999. Central to the Trust's ambitions was the reconstruction of Colossus, described as the world's first programmable computer, brilliantly devised in the early 1940s by Tommy Flowers, a post office engineer, but completely destroyed at the end of the war together with all other evidence of Bletchley's activities. Tony Sale, an electronics engineer, not only successfully achieved this reconstruction (completed in 2007), but also served as the Trust's Secretary and was appointed the Trust's security liaison officer.

By then, in 1993, the first formal reunion of Y-Branch operators had assembled at Bletchley, some half-century after the activity that had formed their joint experience. Of course, small groups of friends had always kept in social touch, and there was an active 'Tels(S) Association', largely composed of operators formerly working in the Far East, but the Bletchley Reunion was a formally organized occasion covering all activities pursued at Bletchley, with lectures and much exchange of information. The following year, in the autumn of 1994, the Second Reunion attracted some 250 veterans, who enjoyed a weekend of talks that widened many restricted horizons. The Trust, through Tony Sale, was now actively seeking reminiscences from veterans, and authority to talk was sought from GCHQ, who in December 1994 gave qualified approval, notifying us that "the dispensation from the obligation of confidentiality (under the Official Secrets Act) about your work relates only to this undertaking and to discussions about it with Mr Sale", who was himself bound to use documentary material only as authorized by GCHQ's security officer. Since we, on the listening stations, knew absolutely nothing about Colossus, this dispensation did little to liberate us.

In January 1999, acknowledging considerable help from the Bletchley Park Trust, Channel Four broadcast a four-episode series on 'Station X'. This remarkably explicit account, still available on YouTube, included fascinating contributions from well-placed participants, German as well as British. Surely there was nothing within our deliberately limited experience left to protect?

Another decade was to pass before official liberation finally arrived. In July 2009 came the announcement that a commemorative medal was to be issued to all who had worked at Bletchley Park and its outstations. The letter inviting us to apply included an invitation to "write down any memories you have of your time working in Signals Intelligence. You may consider anything that happened before VJ Day as unclassified". No archive material had survived the post-war expurgation. There was no record of what life was like, whether at Bletchley or on the Y stations. What hours did we work? What were our working conditions like? How did we occupy our free time? What kind of people were we? I began to put my recollections together.

Long ago, shortly after the war, I had written an account of a rather different narrative, the story of how the Royal Navy took a gaggle of young green schoolgirls and turned us into useful naval ratings. To give context to our adventures, I had made guarded references to what we were doing, and since this touched on classified material, I submitted the text to the Admiralty for clearance. It was not given. The text was duly relegated to the back of the proverbial drawer. That document, rather than an exceptionally good tenth-decade memory, is the source of the events of almost seventy years ago here described, supplemented by the material consigned to paper only after 2009.

My medal—in truth a lapel brooch—duly arrived, together with a certificate. It stated: *The Government wishes to express to you its deepest gratitude for the vital service you performed during World War II*, and was signed by Gordon Brown, the then Prime Minister.

I was astonished. What did 'The Government' have to do with it? We had not joined up to serve Mr. Chamberlain, or Mr. Attlee, or even Mr. Churchill, so why did their successors think they were in a position to thank us? We had made our oath of allegiance to the Sovereign, as a symbol of the Nation and all it stood for. 'King and Country' was not an idle phrase. I remembered a day in the summer of 1941, wandering in the Nadder Valley in Wiltshire, when the sun was warm and the fields golden to harvest, and knowing for sure that I would die before I would consent to see Nazi jackboots bestriding that farmland. It had nothing to do with 'The Government'. It would not have been so strange if the citation had said '*Her Majesty's* Government', suggesting the politicians were, alongside us, serving the Nation as personified by the Monarch, but that's not what it said. For 30p I found a suitable frame in the local charity shop, and hung my certificate in the downstairs loo.

Clearly, in the many decades that have passed since WWII, there has been a sea-change in the Nation's political mindset. And not only in politics. These reminiscences bristle with attitudes and assumptions that will seem alien to many today. *Autres temps, autres mœurs.* Let the following pages stand as a testimonial to a world that, for better or worse, is long gone.

A Salted Innocence

It was in 1930 that I first left home to go to sea. I was seven years old.

The cook had scolded me for being under her feet in the kitchen. My mother was busy entertaining visitors in the drawing-room. My little sister threw water from the cold tap at me, so I threw scalding water from the hot tap at her, but she screamed and made a fuss, and when the cook and the nursery-maid heard what had happened, they consoled her and scolded me, which was patently unfair, since she had started the whole thing. There had been several incidents like that, and it was clear to me that everyone preferred my sister to me. There was nothing for it but to run away to sea, like the cabin boys in the various adventure stories I was reading at the time.

I filled a paper bag with cake. In our household we had bread and butter and jam for tea (after First Piece Plain), and one slice of cake, except on Sundays when we could have two slices of cake, because it was a feast day. Two biscuits counted as one piece of cake. But because I was leaving home for good, I felt I deserved something special. I put no bread and butter in the bag, only cakes. It was as special as the day when the doctor's little son gave a birthday party, and there was on the table *no bread at all*, only cakes and biscuits — a truly memorable birthday party, I still remember the thrill, and it happened over eighty-five years ago.

About a mile and a half from home, half way through the Buckinghamshire village nearest our home, I climbed over

the stile by the village church, and sat among the squidgy
cowpats in a buttercup field. It sloped down to a stream,
where rooks were cawing among pollarded trees. I ate the
cakes.

The clock on the church steeple struck four. The door of
the village school opened, and the children came bursting
noisily out. "They're going home", I thought. In spite of
myself, I felt envious. Their mothers would be waiting for
them at home, with tea. As for me, I did not know quite
where the sea was, I had finished all the cake, and I had
nothing to take with me into my new life but an empty
paper bag.

I swallowed my pride and went home. The great gesture
had passed unnoticed. Tea was waiting on the nursery table,
and no one even asked where I had been.

Eleven years later, for rather different reasons, I tried
again. This time there was no going back, and I ate my tea in
the WRNS training establishment in Plymouth. I had
become a probationary Wren.

Chapter I

Sea Fever

So I started to scrub.

If there had been no war, I might have gone to Switzerland to be Finished. I needed it. But instead I went into the Navy, so naturally I took up scrubbing.

Later in the war, initial training for Wrens became complex and highly organized, but at the start of 1942 only two things were required: a reasonable proficiency at squad drill, and a superior proficiency at scrubbing. I loved both. My hands grew raw and the knuckles cracked as I scrubbed and scrubbed in the January cold. I did not mind. I had always known that the Navy scrubbed its decks, and that is exactly what I scrubbed — decks. Of course at boarding school we had called them floors, and if anyone scrubbed them it must have been the maids, but that little change in nomenclature made all the difference.

There were snags of course. There was, for instance, the Spiral Scrub, and a Probationary Wren called Rosemary was caught in its convolutions on the very first day. She scrubbed along the skirting boards right round the room, and then proceeded in diminishing circles until she found she was trapped on a little dry island in the centre with no escape and nowhere to kneel while she scrubbed the remaining dry patch.

But we learnt. I broadened my knowledge of naval terminology by learning the names of all the rooms through which we scrubbed — the fo'c's'le, the galley, the cabins, the Mess. I became an Instructor Scrubber, showing even newer recruits how it was done. I carried coals, waited at table, and did a great deal of washing-up, though the washing-up was not strictly speaking necessary, at least not to the extent to which I indulged in it. The trouble was that quite often the stewards burst into the fo'c's'le after meals and said "Volunteers for washing-up". The old hands among the Wrens continued to sit in their chairs (recliner, ratings, for the use of), knees nonchalantly crossed, fingers tapping the ash from a cigarette, for all the world as if they had not heard what the stewards had said. Whilst I gazed uncertainly from them to the stewards and back again, one of the stewards would invariably catch my eye, and I would find myself in the galley washing-up. But there were compensations, as I found the thick scum of bacon grease on the washing-up water hugely comforting to my broken hands. Anyway, the day came when the stewards amended their techniques, and burst in saying "Volunteers for washing-up—you, you and you—not you", accompanied by clear pointed signals, with the last two words often directed at me; recognition for my days of hard labour.

It was two weeks and two days since I had left school. On the morning that school broke up, all the other girls had stood on the Up platform of our wayside country station (we had been evacuated to Somerset) going home for the holidays; I stood alone on the Down platform, going to Devonport Barracks to join the Navy. For eighteen months I had been waiting for this moment.

It all began because of Captain Scott, the South Pole and a ship called *RRS Discovery*. Several polar crazes were engulfing schoolgirls just before the war, and loyalties were passionately divided between the Arctic, with Gino Watkins for its hero, and the Antarctic, which included Scott and Shackleton sub-factions. They joined the list of linked public figures: Clark Gable and Gary Cooper, for instance; or the Duchess of Kent versus the Duchess of Gloucester, under whose names we divided to play the lazy cricket matches that whiled away the long Saturday evenings of the summer term.

I belonged to the Scott faction. I read every book I could find about Captain Scott's expeditions, and from them it was a short jump to books about the Royal Navy. For some reason our school library was well supplied with books about the Navy, not just fiction by Taffrail and Bartimeus, but there was also the diary of a midshipman sent to sea at the age of thirteen when Dartmouth was mobilized in 1914, and by the age of fifteen a survivor from a warship lost at the Dardanelles; there was a thick volume about the Battle of Cape Coronel, which would have been a very obscure piece of history but for the fact that the victorious German admiral was Graf Spee, and even as I sat in the silent library with the book open on the long, light oak table, the sailors of *HM Ships Exeter, Ajax* and *Achilles* were marching through London in celebration of their victory over the German pocket-battleship that bore his name — a victory in those same Latin-American waters that had earlier brought fame to the admiral. And there was a whole series of books by a naval padre with evocative titles like *In the Northern Mists* and *Grand Fleet Days*, full of simple, rather sentimental poems, over which I shed a tear or two. Anyway, I was born under Pisces, the sign of the sailor, so that settled it, I was going to join the Navy.

I said as much to my best friend.

"Don't be silly", she said, "Join the Army. It's always the Army that matters in the end. You know, the infantry and all that. It's the Army every time for me."

"I don't see why," I said, "specially seeing as both your brothers are in the Navy. Let's both volunteer for the WRNS."

"No", said Mary. "I want to join the Army."

"You'll look awful in khaki."

"Oh well, of course if you're going to decide what to join just according to the colour of the uniform ..."

So we quarrelled and went our separate ways, she to the Army, where she drove the big convoy lorries, and I to the Navy, where ... but that was later.

On my school pencil box were painted two sailors dancing a hornpipe, and a rather distorted battleship. The distortion was not due to bad painting—she was *HMS Rodney*, originally designed as a 48,000-ton ship, but modified to the 35,000-ton limit stipulated in the Treaty of Washington. In final form she had much too much fore and too little aft, but it was just as well, as otherwise she would have gone right off the edge of my pencil box. My school pyjamas I had had specially designed with bell-bottomed trousers, but this had proved a mistake, as they were very draughty when, in the days before the school evacuated to quieter areas, we had had to run about the school grounds at night, taking cover during air-raid alarms. In the end I took to going to bed with bicycle clips on my ankles, a mild device compared with one of my school friends, who wore her wellington boots in bed, so as to be ready in case there was a night dash to the shelters.

In May 1940, in the week of Dunkirk, our school moved west rather hurriedly. We left our red brick buildings on the bleak East Coast, and they were immediately occupied by the Army, who were reputed to be burning the furniture. We found shelter in a Stately Home in Somerset, where Virginia creeper covered the outer walls and Versailles tapestries the inner. There were cedars and copper beeches in the parkland, and rambling stone walls. There was a sunken garden, overlooked by the great State Rooms in which we slept, and lawns on which we played tennis until the petrol for the mowers was exhausted, and we had to rely on horses to nibble the grass short.

The war passed us by. Our request to be allowed to form a rifle brigade whose duty would be to take pot-shots at German paratroops descending on the school roof was not given a sympathetic hearing by the staff. The most we achieved was that the sixth form were trained to cope with incendiary bombs, and we put out one of two practice fires with stirrup pumps. We took it in turns to go on the roof as firewatchers whenever there was a night alarm, but no bombs, incendiary or otherwise, ever came anywhere near us. As a home for an evacuated school, that village must have been ideal.

Others of my age were doing war work, but our only contribution was to thin the beet in some nearby fields. Several of my school friends who had left were in the Forces. They came back to see us, sometimes on forty-eight-hour leave passes, wearing their uniforms. They went to dances, and to the cinema. They even had boy friends.

But we had no contact with the world outside school. At the village church, where we sat in rows strictly segregated from the rest of the congregation, we could see, but not of course ever speak to, the Home Guard. We studied, we played hockey, we walked in the innocuous fields, and for entertainment we danced in the panelled hall of our Stately Home, with its chandelier and tapestries, and family crests. We danced with one another, and took it in turns to lead. For the Christmas dance, the staff and the matrons came too.

I had a tiny little lifeline to the outside world, but no one knew about it. I was keeping up a clandestine correspondence with a soldier in the Duke of Wellington's Regiment. He and I had met during the holidays when we simultaneously leapt for shelter into a ditch full of stinging nettles during a rather unaccountable German raid on adjacent beet fields (I was in Lincolnshire visiting now ex-school friend Mary). But the correspondence languished. I had not admitted I was a schoolgirl, I had said I was a journalist on a Somerset paper, and then salved my conscience by reflecting that I did edit the school magazine. But it proved almost impossible to write letters not mentioning school when that was in fact my entire life. The correspondence petered out, and once more my horizons extended only as far as the leather books locked behind grills in the Earl's library that served us for a prefects' room.

Ever since my seventeenth birthday I had been pleading
to be allowed to join the WRNS, but at that age one had to
have one's parents' permission, and mine, like most parents,
wanted me to finish my schooling first. Finally we struck a
bargain. If I would stay at school long enough to take my
university entrance exams, they would raise no more
objections to my joining up, though I would still be two
years under conscription age, which at that time was twenty
for girls. As my father pointed out, I might win a scholarship
that might be held for me till after the war, or I might change
my mind (no chance) or the war might end (my secret night-
mare). Of course once I turned eighteen I could join without
parental permission, but agreeing to do the exams meant I
would go with their blessing.

So I pondered over the character of Hamlet and learned
by heart my own translations of Xenophon and Virgil. My
only hope of doing well in Greek and Latin exams was to
find a sentence that I recognized, fit it into the translation I
already knew by heart, and work backwards and forwards
from there. The method worked well, and my set book
results always pulled up my weak grammar results to a
reasonable average.

As the Oxford and Cambridge entrance exams drew
near, our studies intensified. Drawing, dancing and singing
were dropped from our timetable, and I spent no more time
on the hockey pitch. I took up Anglo-Saxon, read Beowulf in
the original, and practised writing papers on such subjects as
"The gerund has become an extremely supple means of sub-
ordinating ideas; discuss", a statement which at the time
conveyed very little to my mind, and now conveys nothing.
In any case, it did not seem to me to matter in the least. In
my private history of the War at Sea, I noted that the Royal
Navy had sunk six ships in the Mediterranean and damaged
four more.

Month by month, since September 1939, I had written naval history into my cigarette card album. It was called Modern Naval Craft, issued by Players Cigarettes, price 1d,* and I had collected the whole set (from adults, usually my father, who was a heavy smoker. I was of course not then a smoker myself). Ships of all the principal maritime nations were included. Number Six was *HMS Exeter*, and above her picture I had written an account of her fight against the *Graf Spee*. The *Graf Spee* was in too, Number Twenty-Four, and above her was written tersely "scuttled, Dec.1939, to avoid capture after fight with *Ajax, Exeter* and *Achilles*". Within eighteen months of the start of the war I had had to cross Numbers Nine, Eleven and Twelve from the book, for, of the ships illustrated, *HMShips Curlew, Grenville* and *Afridi* had all gone down, and I had sadly noted the number of casualties each suffered. I made a note of even minor incidents if any-one had been hurt—for instance, by Number Eight, *HMS Southampton*, was written: "Hit by splinters in air-raid on Firth of Forth. About thirteen casualties."

And then on May 24th, *HMS Hood* was sunk. She was Number Four in the album. There in my cigarette card she rode on a spumey painted sea, 42,000 tons of her, with the white ensign flying out from her stern. Above the card in my album I wrote, "Sunk, blew up owing to hit in magazine while fighting *Bismarck* off Greenland. Very few men saved." Her complement, according to the card, had been 1341. But I could not join up to avenge her. I had promised to stay at school.

---

* 'd' stood for denarius. The coinage that Europe inherited from the Roman Empire consisted primarily of the denarius ('d'), 12 of which made up the solidatus ('s'), with 20 solidati (240 denarii) composing 1 libra ('L' or '£'). King Offa of Mercia introduced the system into his Anglo-Saxon kingdom in the Eighth Century, and £sd later became the currency of the newly-established kingdom of England, with the local names of pounds, shillings and pence. The system was marvellously flexible, lasting until decimalization in 1971.

So there was not much I could do but knit gloves and balaclava helmets. I also gathered sweet chestnuts in the school grounds, and posted them to a motor torpedo boat for the crew to roast at the engine room fire, because all my reading about the Navy was of World War I books, I did not know about diesel engines, and I was under the impression that much of the Navy's time was still spent coaling ship and building up huge fires in the boiler room.

At last the time came to sit the entrance exams for Oxford and Cambridge, and afterwards I was called to Cambridge for an interview. Among the schoolgirls staying at Girton College was one who had done the same papers as I had, and we began to compare notes. We had both, for instance, tackled the essay on 'Camouflage'. It was a subject to which I had warmed. After disposing rapidly of the army exchanging its red coats for khaki so as to melt into the veldt during the Boer War, I went on to expound on the Q-ships and the zebra stripes painted on warships during what we still called the Great War.

"Yes", said my new friend. "And then of course there's *mental* camouflage." She said it in a carefully casual tone, but I knew she was scrutinizing me to see if I had thought of that one.

"Of course", I said.

But I knew then that I would never get into Cambridge. I had never for one moment thought of anything so subtle as *mental* camouflage. I was truly sorry. I did not want to go to Cambridge, but for the sake of those who had worked on me so hard, I had hoped to be offered a place. And since August 1939, when my father's Territorial battalion had been embodied, my school fees had been coming from a junior army officer's pay; there was no longer a maid at home. It was disappointing to realize that I had not been worth all the effort people had made for me.

I began the round of interviews. I tried to think intelligently about the relationship between T.S. Eliot and the metaphysical poets. The third don to see me asked a simple question.

"Tell me," she said, "why do you want to come to Cambridge?"

"Oh I don't", I assured her. "I want to join the WRNS."

There was a moment's silence.

"Well", she said at last, and quite kindly. "I'm sure you would do very useful work. You would be an officer, I suppose, so your good education would not be wasted."

I returned to school. Oxford had decided, in view of the chaotic transport disruption caused by bombing, not to hold interviews, but to award places on the basis of the written papers only. There was nothing more for me to do at my books.

And then came the news that *Prince of Wales* and *Repulse* had been sunk off Malaya. *Repulse* was Number Five in my album. No promises now stood in my way, and a week later I was on the train for Devonport.

There was a Navy man in my carriage that day as I travelled from school to join up. I took him for an officer, since he was wearing a navy blue suit and peaked cap, not the traditional bell-bottomed trousers and sailor cap, a distinction that I was later to learn covered, in those days, the difference between the Seamanship categories in Square Rig, and the Clerical categories (like Pay Clerks) who, together with non-commissioned officers of the rank of petty office and above, wore Fore and Aft Rig. I confided to him that I was on my way to join the Navy, whereupon he took me under his wing, got me off the train at the right stop, put me on the right bus, and … paid for my bus fare. This last detail worried me. I wondered if it was wrong to let a strange man, even if he was in the Navy, buy my bus ticket. I wondered what my mother would say about it. I offered to repay him, but he would not hear of it.

Soon we came to *HMS Drake*, the Royal Naval Barracks, Devonport, and for the first time in my life I set foot in a naval establishment. Just inside the gates a tear-gas demonstration was in progress, and somehow I became involved in it, which pleased me, as it made me feel at once that my sheltered school days were over, and I was now grown up and emancipated. I groped my way, my eyes streaming, into the building where the WRNS had their administrative headquarters. It seemed for a moment to be rather like school again, there was the same green paint and the same smell of disinfectant soap. But there was also a significant difference — wielding a pail of water and squee-gee in the corridor was a real sailor, in a real sailor's uniform, and with a hat on his head. It struck me as odd that he should be wearing his hat indoors.

A WRNS officer interviewed me.

"What category are you interested in?" she said.

I was not quite sure what a category was.

"Well," she said, "what did you think you would like to do in the WRNS?"

I was not very sure about this either. I had heard vaguely of something called 'plotters', and accordingly I suggested I might be a plotter.

"I'm afraid there are no vacancies for plotters," said the officer, "there's a long waiting list. Never mind, I suggest you come along anyway, and join up, and then we'll think what you should do afterwards. What is your civilian job?"

"I left school this morning."

"Splendid!" she said, "Then you can come at once."

Keen though I was, I had not expected anything quite as sudden as this.

"Do you think", I said, "that I could go home and say goodbye to my parents? It was boarding-school, you see, and my trunk is on the train now, going home, and I ought to go and unpack it."

She quite saw the point. Then she remembered it was Christmas in a few days, so she suggested I should go home for Christmas, and come along back to Devonport after-wards. Meanwhile I must see the MO and pass the medical.

Medicals for would-be recruits were to be held the next day, so I was sent to spend the night in one of the WRNS quarters in Plymouth. It was one of the advantages of boarding-school life—at any rate in evacuated conditions which were usually overcrowded and lacking in privacy— that stripping off my clothes and going to bed in full view of other girls held no terrors for me. I had long ago lost all modesty of that kind. For girls who had never so much as shared a bedroom before, it was an ordeal, but for me it was just like school. I was given the bed of a Wren who had gone on night watch, and I snuggled down delirious with happiness. Only twenty-four hours ago I had been in my bed at school—a schoolgirl. Now I was very nearly a Wren.

Very nearly—but not quite. During the night I had leisure to think about it. Plymouth was still under sporadic attack, though the main devastation had occurred a few weeks previously, and that night there was an air-raid. The Wren officers woke us, and sent us to shelter. I sat in the dark, and worried about my eyesight. I was short-sighted, and I was not sure I could pass the test.

Next day I was taken back to the Barracks and deposited in the Medical Block. All went well so long as all I had to do was jump on and off chairs, breathe deeply, and confess to chicken-pox and tonsillitis in childhood. But then there was no more avoiding the real problem. I walked to the Eye Block and opened the door.

Inside the door was a long passage leading away to my right, and on my left another door obviously leading to the sight-testing room. All down both sides of the narrow passage were benches, and all down the benches sat Seamen, hundreds of them. Still in my school coat, I made my anxious way along the neat lines of dark blue serge with the clean collars and smart triple bands of white until at the end of one of the benches I found a space, and sat down.

We sat and we sat and we sat. Nobody spoke. Nothing happened. I heard a click as the door of the testing room opened, but I did not look up; my turn would not come for a long while. Next moment, I was in a heap on the floor. The bench on the end of which I had been sitting had see-sawed. Every Seaman was standing rigidly to attention, and there was no longer any weight to balance mine on the bench.

From the floor I looked up. I was at the feet of a magnificent naval officer, covered in more gold braid than I had ever seen before. Several more officers stood behind him, one even seemed to have gold ropes hung round his shoulders. Beyond them on either side stretched rigid lines of silent, poker-faced Seamen.

I picked myself up.

"I'm awfully sorry", I said, too ignorant even to add the obligatory "Sir".

"That's quite all right", said the officer. And that was how I met the Commodore of R.N. Barracks, Devonport. It was not an auspicious start to my naval career. The little procession re-formed, gathered momentum, and steamed away down the passage, round the corner and out of sight. We all sat down on the benches again. And went on sitting. I hoped one of the large Seamen beside me would say something friendly, so that I could feel I might be acceptable in a Naval Establishment in spite of this bad start, but nobody spoke.

At last it was my turn. I was not wearing my glasses, as I did not want to put ideas into the examiner's head, but I looked quickly at the board, and, with both eyes at once, memorized as much as I could. But there was not time to learn sufficient letters, and obviously I was considered marginal, because I was sent for a supplementary test to a very explosive commander. His final explosion was worth waiting for.

"You pass", he said, and then added, "Just."

So everything seemed to be settled, and all I had to do was go home and wait for my call-up papers. At last, at long, long last, I was going to join the Navy.

But when I got home there was a telegram waiting for me. It came from an Oxford college, Lady Margaret Hall, and it offered me a vacancy for the following academic year. My father stood with the telegram in his hand. The chance of a lifetime was being offered to me — only about one in ten of those who sat the exams was offered a place.

My father stuck to our bargain. He did not try to influence me, though I knew how much he had always wanted to give his children the chance of the Oxbridge education that he had never had.

"I'm joining up", I said.

He understood. It was what he had done in 1914, and again, in March 1939, when, realizing that war was inevitable, he had rejoined his old Territorial Regiment. He wrote to LMH enquiring if the place could be saved for after the war, but was told that was impossible when places for women at Oxford were so restricted, there would be unknown numbers in my position, and nothing was known as to whether there would be any relaxation of the restriction on numbers at the war's end.

On January 1st, 1942, two weeks after leaving school, my railway warrant for travel to Devonport arrived. That day, in the middle of cutting up a fine toad-in-the-hole, my mother suddenly remembered an old music hall song which she had heard in her early Edwardian childhood. Waving the carving knife at me so that no one would mistake her meaning, or her reason for bursting into song, she suddenly sang:

Birdie wait a little longer

Till the little wings are stronger …

But she couldn't remember any more. So the next day I caught the train for Devonport again; and Drake's drum was throbbing in my ears.

Chapter II
Devonport Days

When we were not scrubbing, we had a few lectures. The mysteries of naval terminology were unravelled for us, and from then on we called our knives and forks by the extraordinary name of 'mess traps'. An embarrassed medical officer gave us a talk called 'Hygiene'. In part it was about nits and head lice, and then I got embarrassed too, because I should not have known anything about them, but I did, because in the turmoil of evacuation some of them had turned up at school, no one knew whence. We had had to have head inspections every day (oh, the *shame* of it), and be soaked in paraffin if anything suspicious turned up. I had been soaked in paraffin myself, because I was suspected of harbouring a dead egg, but one of my friends had positively boasted that she had got two eggs, both new-laid. I hoped that none of the recruits could tell from my face that I knew all about nits—*pediculi humani* we had been taught to call them at school.

Then the MO went on to other subjects which seemed to embarrass him far more, but me far less. It was all about behaving ourselves, and seemed to me quite unnecessary. If he gave us any information on VD it must have gone right over my head. I don't remember becoming aware of that topic until later in the year, when we were bombarded with films, even in the commercial cinema, and advertisements in every newspaper emblazoned with the slogan "Clean Living is the Only Real Safeguard!".

To all our lectures we listened with an earnest and help-ful attention. One evening an R.N. Lieutenant spoke to us on the very general subject of 'The Royal Navy'.

"What", he asked the class, "is the first requirement of the Navy?"

A moment of speculation, and then a hand went up.

"The sea?" suggested a recruit.

Then there were lectures on security and careless talk. These made a profound impression on me. A month later I went home on my first forty-eight-hour pass. In my carriage on the train were a group of matelots who wanted to know where I was stationed, what I did, and a hundred other questions. I remembered that lecture on security, and to everything they asked me I said "I don't know". When I got off the train, one of them leaned wearily out of the carriage window to wave me goodbye.

"And for God's sake", he shouted after me, "try to learn *something* about *something*."

There were also the gas lectures. It was the first subject with which we were confronted on joining up, before we had even begun squad drill or scrubbing. The first Petty Officer to talk to us on this subject had no front teeth and spoke very indistinctly, but enough came across to make us all feel sick with fear at the very thought of a poison gas attack. At the end of his talk, he announced that he was now going to let off some tear gas.

"But first," he said, "Leading Seaman Brown here will go round and take a note of your next-of-kin and their tele-phone numbers."

It was no good. We were beyond the reach of jocularity. There were a few wan smiles, but several Probationary Wrens did not even realize it was a joke.

When the two weeks probationary training were up, we were enrolled for the duration of 'Hostilities Only' (making us 'HOs'). I was given an official number, 31872, which I shared with a steam engine running on the Great Western line, and I signed a paper saying that I knew I should be thrown out if I disobeyed my officers. I received 13s a week in pay, which fairly soon went up to 15s.

It seemed plenty. A shampoo and set cost only 3s. Canteen dances were free, and in some canteens you could eat and drink as much tea as you wanted for 6d – though these were usually church canteens, and one was apt to be let in for a Word of God as well. Where religion was concerned I was a traditionalist, and did not feel at home with God too cosily mixed up with the currant buns.

It was in one of the canteens that I gazed in astonishment at a soldier and a Wren who were apparently dancing – but the soldier spent his time flinging the girl rhythmically half across the floor. It was not at all like ballroom dancing at school, not even like 'swing', a jerky little foxtrot which we had learnt in the belief that it was quite the latest thing.

"They're jiving", someone told me. "It's not allowed at the Hammersmith Palais. A sailor threw a girl in the air and forgot to catch her when she came down. She hit her head and died."

"Terrible memories sailors have", said someone else.

Uniforms were not issued to us until our two weeks as Probationary Wrens were completed. I had never had adult civilian clothes. I had been making my school clothes last, so that I could burst into new clothes when I left school, like a butterfly from its chrysalis, but I had been caught out by clothes rationing, which was introduced during my last term, so all I possessed when I joined up, apart from a gym slip, were a few sensible skirts and jerseys. Instead of bursting from a chrysalis, I merely exchanged one navy blue uniform for another, but no debutante could have been prouder of her coming-out dress than I was of my blue serge suit and pudding-bowl hat. I had no trouble tying my tie – we had worn house ties at school, and I knew how to do it, but the starched shirt collars bothered me, and raised red weals on my neck. Black lisle stockings were provided, and 'black-outs', stout navy knickers which no euphemisms could glamorize. One Wren read aloud a letter from her boyfriend, consoling her over these garments with the remark that in wartime all places of amusement must be blacked out. It was quite the rudest Rude Joke I had ever heard in my life. I was shocked.

I had a gold wire hat ribbon saying *HMS Drake*, and I polished it with bread crumbs to make it shine. I tied the bow the way the old salts showed me, with an old silver threepenny bit inside the knot to make it tiddly. That was about all the scope there was for feminine vanity.

There was a certain Petty Officer in the training establishment who indulged her femininity by wearing black silk stockings. These were permitted off-duty, but we could not acquire them, as we had no coupons ('clothing chits' enabling us to buy underclothes and stockings from civilian shops were not issued until later in the war). The Petty Officer's secret supply was her pre-Service civilian silk stockings, which she had dyed black. I sighed with envy. I had only my school lisle, and even they were patched, to get me through my last term.

On going into uniform, 'Salutes and Marks of Respect' ceased to be a lecture subject, and became a practical problem. I wore my uniform for the first time on a Sunday, and went where the problems were thickest, Devonport Barracks, where we were to go to church. A group of three of us were standing waiting to go down to the parade ground, when I saw approaching us a very senior naval officer. The other two had their backs to him. I wanted to tell them he was coming but my mind was too preoccupied with working out the etiquette of the situation. We were not under cover, so someone should salute. But one of my companions was a Leading Wren, and there was something in the instructions about the senior rating present being the only one to salute. No — that was when one was fallen in, and we were not fallen in. As for the salute itself, elbow must be back in line with the shoulder, forearm straight, no hump at the wrist, hand angled so that the palm was not visible from the front, thumb aligned accurately with side of hand … By this time the admiral was abreast of us, and as I had not taken my eyes off him for some moments he could tell that some momentous Mark of Respect was brewing within me. I stood to attention, and the admiral's hand began to move to return my salute. Unfortunately, my hand and arm would not obey me. I could not bring myself to make this funny gesture called a salute. As the admiral was half way through his acknowledgement he had, after an almost imperceptible moment of hesitation, to finish it. So it ended up with my failing to salute anyone, but being saluted by an admiral.

We naturally soon became very blasé about saluting. In the Barracks, we saluted all officers, but outside we were only bound to salute WRNS officers, and naval officers of flag rank. We extended this slightly, and saluted other naval officers if they were particularly handsome, or if it looked as if their morale was sagging and they needed cheering up. My salutes were very smart, but a nuisance to the officers, because I was too vain to wear my glasses, and by the time I had made up my mind whether this was a case in which I should or should not salute, I was practically past the victim of my Mark of Respect. I never did discover how anyone, with or without glasses, could decide whether a young man in officer's cap and a raincoat was a sub-lieutenant (to be saluted) or a midshipman (not to be saluted). It all depended really on whether he looked as if he was through the spotty stage, in which case he probably warranted a salute.

And then, of course, there was squad drill. We had been marched through the Barracks to that gas lecture on our very first day, but it had been a motley affair, as we knew nothing about marching, and anyway we were in civilian clothes, some with high heels and little hats with feathers in them. On the parade ground at the training establishment we took up squad drill in earnest. Then we were sent back to the Barracks for a polishing at the hands of a gunnery instructor.

We fell in in front of him in the drill shed, and he gave us a ten minute tongue-lashing. Constantly and consistently, he said, the Wrens disgraced the Navy. We were sloppy, slack, undisciplined and incompetent. Very soon we should be required to march in public, when the Warship Week parades began, and he was going to see to it that if we disgraced ourselves it should be through no fault of his.

"Wren Squad", he finished up in a bellow, "----" and then he emitted a most incredible sound of what we took to be concentrated disapproval and contempt. It was a sort of breathy groan, emitted through the nose. We gaped at him. He did exactly the same thing all over again, even more angrily.

"Wren Squad. MMMMM." Suddenly someone had an idea. She moved her two feet together. The idea caught on. Pretty soon we had all come smartly, though in individual timing, to attention. Training for Warship Week had begun.

A rash of these parades was about to break out across the West Country. The First Lord of the Admiralty Mr. A.V. Alexander, Mr. Hore-Belisha, and sundry admirals kept popping up to take the salute and make speeches exhorting us to give our money to the Government so that they could buy battleships. Prominent citizens set the ball rolling with generous purchases of war bonds, but some people said they cashed them again the next week and then did it all over again for Tanks and Aeroplanes. But we were much moved, and began buying small saving stamps each pay day in the hope that some day we should have enough stamps to exchange them for a whole 15s savings certificate. By saving a steady ten per cent of our pay, we could accomplish this feat in about three months.

The first town to put us on parade was Tiverton. At the top of the town we fell in—the band of the Royal Marines, the armed guard of Seamen, the Wrens and the naval cadets.

"Parade. Into threes. Right turn."

Quietly, no fuss, no stamping, leave that to the Army. We are the Silent Service. Thumbs forward, elbows straight, swing to the top of the hip in front, no higher, leave exaggeration to the Army.

The drums rolled twice, and then there swelled from ahead of us the long, slow, utterly confident notes of the Royal Navy's march,

Now cheer up my lads …

Sunlight gleamed on the rifle barrels ahead, hypnotically the white gaiters rose and fell, the rolling flap of bell-bottoms concealed, for the moment, beneath the ceremonial precision of the guard.

Hearts of oak are our ships,
Jolly tars are our men …

I should never hear that music again without being aware of rough blue serge, steps in unison, and a great underlying sense of security.

At the bottom end of the town we were told that tea had been prepared for us at the top of town, so we marched back up again, but not to *Hearts of Oak* or the Royal Marines own *Life on the Ocean Wave*, as this was an unofficial march, and anyway it was uphill, and the Marines were out of breath.

It was mid-afternoon. A large church hall was waiting for us, and we filed in and sat down. In front of each of us was one dry roll and a glass of water, which was very disappointing, as we had hoped for a cup of tea and a sugar bun. We were beginning to crumble our dry rolls, when a door opened, and waitresses appeared, carrying plates of roast beef, Yorkshire pudding and two veg. Afterwards came spotted dick and tea, and civic dignitaries who thanked us for coming, and offered us cigarettes and even, for the matelots, cigars. We had a very good time, but left wondering whether Warship Week in Tiverton had shown any profit at all.

Next time it was Honiton. We arrived far too early, and the entire parade was taken for a long route march into the countryside. We squeezed our way back into town along an edge-of-town street so narrow that the armed guard ahead of us were able to knock on every door as we went by, leaving a trail of surprised householders answering the doors as we came abreast of them.

But that day we were not given meat and two veg in the middle of the afternoon, and we returned to Devonport hungry. Fearing we had missed supper in the Wrennery in Plymouth, we decided to try and cadge a meal from the Seamen's Mess in the Barracks, and, in the pitch dark of a winter's night, we fell in behind the Seamen and set off across the Barracks.

We marched for so long that we became suspicious. Besides, the Seamen were marching with a longer stride than we could manage without splitting the seams of our skirts, and we were falling behind. We broke into a trot, caught up with the rear trio of Seamen, and asked where they were going. They were the crew of a famous warship, and they were on their way to the dockyard to go aboard her. In the darkness of the blacked-out Barracks we had fallen in behind the wrong squad. So we went supperless to bed.

But I was far too happy to mind. I belonged, I belonged, I belonged. On my first home leave I was with my mother in Salisbury when a sailor, approaching on the same pavement, called "'lo Jenny" as he passed me. "'lo Jack", I responded. My mother was bemused. "Do you *know* that sailor?" she enquired. "No", I replied. "But I don't have to. We're just both Navy."

Every day at Divisions I heard the Naval Prayer read — that prayer for the Fleet "in which we serve".

O Eternal Lord God, who alone spreadest out the heavens, and rulest the raging of the sea; who has compassed the waters with bounds until day and night come to an end: Be pleased to receive into thy Almighty and most gracious protection the persons of us thy servants, and the Fleet in which we serve. Preserve us from the dangers of the sea, and from the violence of the enemy; that we may be a safeguard unto our most gracious sovereign Lord, King George, and his Dominions, and a security for such as pass on the seas upon their lawful occasions; that the inhabitants of our Island may in peace and quietness serve thee our God; and that we may return in safety to enjoy the blessings of the land, with the fruits of our labours; and with a thankful remembrance of thy mercies to praise and glorify thy holy Name; through Jesus Christ our Lord.

Eternal Lord God. Eternal—yesterday, today and tomorrow. The prayer brought with it that same sense of sureness, of certainty, of confidence, of security, that lingered also among the unsubtle notes of *Hearts of Oak*. Others might pray to Almighty God, and if sufficiently surprised would turn Him round and say 'God Almighty!'. But the Royal Navy prayed to the Eternal Lord God.

Eternal. The word was there again in the hymn so specially associated with the Navy.

Eternal Father strong to save
Whose arm doth bind the restless wave,
Who bidd'st the mighty ocean deep
Its own appointed limits keep,
O hear us when we cry to Thee
For those in peril on the sea.

Over and over again throughout the war we were to hear those words. Many churches ended every Sunday's service with a verse of it. Every naval church parade included 'Those in peril on the sea ...'; so many brothers, so many boy-friends were at sea.

To Devonport the big warships came from the world's oceans. In spite of my affection for the Navy, I had never seen a naval ship before I joined up. Some Wrens—stationed inland—never did see one. There was Plymouth Hoe in all its glory—past and present; and there was a house that I found one day quite by accident, a house called 'Outlands'. I knew it from photographs in the books I had read at school: it had been Captain Scott's home in the 1890s.

The fact that I had just been released from boarding school probably accounted for at least part of the cloud of happiness on which I floated. To thumb a lift to the Barracks from a cold and uncomfortable naval transport seemed the very peak of emancipation; and the anonymity of my uniform allowed me to depart from the narrower conventions of my background and indulge in delicious pastimes such as walking along the street on a winter's evening publicly eating, clutched in my woolly gloves, hot chips in newspaper from the fish and chip shop.

Plymouth people were good to us. Private householders invited us to their homes in the evening, and gave us coffee and cake. A Wren who found herself a temporary substitute home and family would take a friend along on the next visit, and next time the friend's friend would come too, until the noble householder might find herself entertaining anything up to a dozen Wrens.

It was in Plymouth, a few weeks before I went there, that the first Wren boat-crews went into training, but it was a category debarred to me because I had not got good enough eyesight. However, there was nothing wrong with my ears, and I had decided to be a wireless telegraphist. I was learning Morse, helped by a Leading Wren who was an ex-telegraphist, but who had changed category because she could not bear sitting still for the hours involved in watch-keeping on a wireless set. A course was due to start in Dundee, but my application was too late, and the course was already full. There was nothing for it but to wait for the next course to begin, so I remained at the training depot, doing any job that came along.

After I had become a proficient scrubber I was trusted with the duties of an officers' steward and was allowed to fill their hot water bottles and make their tea. Unfortunately, a long-standing fault, an inability to pay adequate attention to the concept of Time, reasserted itself. 'Naval time is five minutes before time', we were told over and over again. After the officers' tea had been anything from fifteen to thirty minutes late on several occasions, I was relegated to general duties steward again.

Then for a while I was a messenger, and after that a seamstress, and was told to make curtains for the Wrennery windows. I did not know how to use a sewing machine, but I had realized that in the Navy one did not say "I can't", one just got on with it. A friend of mine became a driver that way, without ever having been taught to drive.

When I had made and hung curtains at all the Wrennery windows, using curtain rods which I salvaged from bombed buildings, I took up painting and distempered a number of rooms.

And then, quite suddenly, I got a draft. I was sent to R.N. Barracks, Devonport, as a 'writer'.

'Writer' was an ambiguous term. It included everything from the most unskilled clerical work to that of a confidential private secretary. It covered some of the most fascinating of all the WRNS jobs and some of the dullest. I was to work for a Wren officer who was responsible for a variety of administrative tasks, including the clothing store and the monthly reports. Occasionally she said 'bloody' (quite racy, at that time, for a female), and she was known to drink whisky. She alarmed me a good deal.

The monthly reports were compiled from statistics submitted by each WRNS establishment in Plymouth Command. They were supposed to show the number of Wrens in each category, in each rank, at each establishment, and the accommodation provided for them. But the figures never tallied. They would, for instance, report fifty Wrens accommodated, and forty-nine employed, and as there was never time, before the Report had to be sent in, to write for explanations of all the discrepancies, I was instructed to "make it come out right", so I could either eliminate a bed or invent an extra steward or driver or visual signaller as the fancy took me. Sometimes the totals seemed to tally, but only because the arithmetic was wrong.

One station persistently reported eight beds less than the number of Wrens on strength, and no amount of juggling with the figures would account for it. We asked for clarification. It was a watch-keeping station, and there were always eight Wrens on night duty. The remainder rotated through the available beds.

In Plymouth itself, the Wrens lived in one place and worked in another, so they were reported from two separate establishments, and it was quite impossible to narrow down where the error was when the numbers failed to tally. Moreover, a number of Plymouth Wrens were 'Immobile', that is to say they lived at home, so they only appeared in the employment statistics.

These reports went to the House of Commons, and were the basis, so I was told, for the decision on how much food and money to allocate to Plymouth Command for payment of its Wrens. Each month I struggled to account for the work and whereabouts of some 3,500 girls, and each month my sense of guilt deepened. What if Parliament discovered that I had been covering up discrepancies in the reports—cooking the books in fact? Would I be reported to Winston Churchill himself, and my whole naval career end in shame and ignominy? In the end, Nemesis was to catch up with me, but not in that form.

It was part of my job to keep the Record Book, containing the names of all the girls who had been enrolled in Plymouth Command. Girls who had to be discharged because they were pregnant had to be crossed off, but there had only been seven illegitimate pregnancies in the whole of Plymouth Command since the start of the war. Occasionally there were desertions, and then the girl's name was struck from the record in red ink, and the word "Run" and the date entered instead.

Quite apart from any question of principle, I could see no sense at all in deserting. Until one owned up to some Authority or other, one had no ration book, and once one did own up and start eating again, it would simply mean that (unless still too young for call-up) one would be conscripted into a factory or back into the Services again.

There was no court-martial for desertion, one simply sank from the record, and the waters closed quietly over one's disgraced head. This was possible because the WRNS was not under the Naval Discipline Act.

We had mixed feelings about this. It could be a source of pride—the ATS and the WAAF had to be brought under their respective Service Discipline Acts because there were so many desertions, but the Wrens were almost all volunteers who loved the Navy and very seldom deserted. But we had a sneaking feeling that it meant the Navy did not quite accept us, and members of the other Services taunted us about it.

When I first reported for work, I was given the rough draft of several letters to send out. There was a typewriter in the office, and although I had never worked one before, I presumed that, as with the sewing machine, now was the time to start. Laboriously I typed out the letters while the wastepaper basket filled with my discarded efforts. At last I achieved what I regarded as success—anyway I knew I had reached the top limit of my ability as a typist. I took them to my officer, who said they were too disgraceful to carry her signature, and from then on our letters went out in my own handwriting with her signature. I did not seem to be making much success of my career as a writer.

I worked with a big jolly girl who cheered me with a hearty "Never mind, eh?" each time my deficiencies were revealed. One day a fierce and authoritative male voice rang up and said, "Tell Third Officer Blank that if she wants to make private phone calls to her friends in Scotland, she's not to do it on Admiralty lines." Anyone with a little more worldly wisdom than I had would have fetched Third Officer Blank to the phone to speak to him in person, but I took the message, put the phone down, and reflected what a terrible thing Devotion to Duty was, as it was going to be very unpleasant indeed to take such a message to Third Officer Blank, who, although she always lost any papers committed to her charge, was quite nice, and had given me several chocolates in the past. I delivered the message, and she never gave me chocolates again. My colleague said "Never mind, eh?"

Worse, much worse, was to follow. On Easter Monday the office had a half holiday. As the youngest and most junior Wren, I was told to remain on duty at the telephone switchboard. The time for silent heroics was past, and I frankly confessed that I did not know how to operate a switchboard. The telephonists reassured me. As there would be very little going on, they had put the switchboard out of action, and everything would come through on one line, which they called the 'Outside Line'. Then they all went home.

At the switchboard all was quiet. Then suddenly a little white convex disc, like an eyelid, fluttered down in one of the spaces along the top of the switchboard. I seized a plug at random, thrust it into a hole at random, and said "Hullo" into every telephone mouthpiece I could find. There were several scattered about the room. But nobody replied, and the eyelid continued to flutter, making a rather disagreeable rasping sound. Very soon a second one began to flutter, and there were two rasping sounds. I tried a few more wires in a few more holes, and spoke into all the phones in turn, but without success. The rasping sound was beginning to annoy me, so I lifted the eyelids with my finger enough to stick pencils under them, and although this did not quite silence the noise it altered the note, which made a change.

Then a number of tiny trap doors down the side of the switchboard came alive. They all popped open and began buzzing. I tried holding them shut, but the minute I let go they popped open again, and went on buzzing. In the end I gave up the struggle, took the pencils out, and let the whole board buzz and rasp as it liked. I propped my chair at an angle against the wall, put my feet up on the table and read a magazine. Ultimately all the activity on the board stopped and there was peace and quiet again.

About half an hour later one of the eyelids again plopped down. I decided to have one more try at answering, and shoved two wires into two holes. By some horrible coincidence I put them in the right places, and found myself speaking to a furious Wren officer, who had spent the entire afternoon trying to make an urgent phone call to Admiralty.

When I explained what had happened, she was sympathetic.

"Stay where you are," she said, "I'll come over and give you instruction."

Unfortunately, she was not the first to think of coming over. By the time she arrived the switchboard room was full of irate officers who seemed to be converging from all over the Barracks. When the situation had been sorted out and I had been properly instructed, they all went back to their offices and rang one another up, or put through difficult calls to distant places like Admiralty, so I became very proficient by the end of the day.

But none of this increasing versatility at work helped me to become socially proficient. For one thing, I did not know how to hold a cocktail glass. I was convinced there was a right and a wrong way depending on what one was drinking (fingers on the stem? Or round the bowl?), and that my social ineptitude would be discovered the moment anyone offered me a drink. I asked one or two people about this, but they seemed to think it did not matter. I did not believe them.

There was in our cabin a Wren despatch rider. She was an extremely experienced motor-cyclist, a dirt-track rider of pre-war fame, but she was very old, over thirty anyway, and we called her Grannie. She had a wide circle of friends in Plymouth, and she decided that we must be introduced to some young men, so she organized a party for us. We were to be escorted by four Midshipmen from the Royal Naval Engineering College. It was to be my first formal social encounter with the opposite sex—I had no brothers, and young men were a closed book to me, so I looked forward to the party with a mixture of excitement and trepidation.

On the morning of the day on which the party was to be held, I received a telegram from my father, saying "Many happy returns and best love". As it was not my birthday, this puzzled me. In a way it was an appropriate message, but as I had not mentioned the proposed party in letters home, I wondered how he could possibly have known about it.

In the evening we were taken by Grannie to a local pub, and introduced to our four Midshipmen. They asked us what we would like to drink. The other girls said "gin and lime", so I said gin and lime too, as the only other drink I knew of was sherry, which I had had at home, but only before meals.

The Midshipmen had pink gins, of which I had never heard. They said that actually they preferred pink gins, actually. We said that actually we preferred gin and lime, actually. After that there did not seem to be anything else to say.

The Midshipmen continued to talk about gin. Then they reminded one another about the time someone called Geoff had got squiffy at someone-or-other's party. Then they each told stories about the times they themselves had got squiffy.

I felt very left out, as I'd never even seen anyone who had got squiffy. I wondered if it would be possible to have a new topic of conversation, but could not think of anything. We had defeated the WAAF at hockey the previous Saturday, and had tea and buns at the YWCA afterwards, but I did not think this would interest them. So I said nothing.

We sat in the pub all evening. I was given a second gin and lime before I had finished the first (I did not like it very much), and a third when I had barely started on the second, although I had said that there was still plenty in my glass. When the pub closed, I had still not started my third gin and lime, which seemed very ungrateful, as Midshipmen got very little pay.

Nevertheless, I could not possibly drink the gin and lime in one hasty gulp. I formed my first Ruthless Rule. If men buy you another drink when you've said you don't want it, then however poor they are, you just leave it. That particular gin and lime was not left, however, as one of the Midshipmen hurriedly drank it.

The evening was not really a great success. On the other hand, no one seemed to notice anything funny about the way I held my cocktail glass. It was a step in the right direction.

About two days later I got another telegram from my father. All it said was "sackcloth and ashes", which puzzled me even more than the first. The explanation emerged later. My father relied on my mother to prompt him about birthdays and anniversaries. But Army life had separated him from my mother, so he was dependent on his own resources. He had tried to visualize the income tax form on which he entered his children as his dependents, with their dates of birth. The telegram had been sent to me on a date which applied to one sister, and month which applied to another. It just happened not to have anything to do with me.

I wrote home about the party. I said I had been a bit disillusioned about men, as they talked about nothing but drinking. My father replied that that was natural in the very young, and they would grow out of it. But I found as time went on that my father was only partly right.

Grannie had no further opportunity to advance my social education. My draft came through. I was to report to a village in Hampshire to begin training as a telegraphist. Ships and the sea were left behind; cows, meadows and the Morse key lay ahead.

First, though, I was to have a week's leave. I went home, and my family were immediately impressed at how my posture had improved. They attributed the improvement to squad drill.

Ever since I was a child, people had nagged me for not standing up straight. When I was about nine years old, my parents decided there must be something wrong with my spine, and took me to a Harley Street specialist. He had looked at my back, and then undone my stocking sus-penders, which in the fashion of the time for little girls were attached to a liberty-bodice, so that I had been hooked in one long loop from shoulder to toe. I had outgrown the stretch of the elastic. After that there had been an improvement, but it had not lasted. We had 'Deportment' every week at school, when we had to march round the hall with books on our heads. Invariably I lost marks for my house by performing such feats as 'leaning backwards with poking chin'. Once I even let the books drop off my head, an unheard of catastrophe, which lost my house two marks at once, and led to everyone whispering about me in corners for several days. I had to go to extra deportment classes every morning before breakfast. But I got no better.

It seemed, however, that at last I had begun to stand up. I don't think it was due to squad drill. I think it was due to sheer happiness, combined with the confident conviction that I belonged to the greatest Navy in the world.

Chapter III

A Pastoral Apprenticeship

Rural is perhaps an inadequate word to describe the next few months. Before they were over we were wondering whether we were training for the Navy or the Land Army. It began with chickens, and it was largely due to the fact that there were about a dozen of us who reported for training from other naval establishments, and about ninety girls 'straight from shore', in other words new recruits, wearing civilian clothes.

'Divisions' at our new 'ship' were held out of doors, and we uniformed Wrens tended to leave it to the new recruits to fill the front ranks. As a result, we could not hear what was said unless the wind was in the right direction. On one particular morning the prayers were obviously followed by a talk, which we could not hear, after which the recruits in front of us put their hands up, so, not wishing to miss any-thing, we also put up our hands. We learnt afterwards that we had voted to buy chickens with the Mess funds.

The Mess fund accrued out of money saved, by careful budgeting, from our provision allowance. It was intended to be used to provide us with extras — a wireless set in the fo'c's'le, for instance, or to cover the expenses of holding a dance. It was our First Officer's suggestion that we should keep chickens, and thus supplement the egg rations. This we had now voted to do.

They must have been incredibly bad layers. Every Sunday a list went up on the board naming the Wrens who could claim an egg for breakfast that day. At the end of four months some of us still had not managed to get on to that list, which was a pity, because it was almost a year after that before we had another boiled egg (and I remember the day very clearly, because I overslept and missed breakfast). Certain subversive voices muttered that the officers had eggs every Sunday.

Our officers certainly seemed very pleased with the hen idea. Shortly afterwards we found we had voted to buy pigs. Then ducks. Then came two goats and a cow. Then a pony and trap in which our CO drove to church on Sundays. It was then suggested that we buy geese.

We came as near to mutiny as we dared. We said we had absolutely no use for geese, and did not wish to buy any.

Our CO sent for the representatives of the Mess committee. She told us that we were the most selfish, self-centred bunch of Wrens it had ever been her misfortune to command. Very shortly we would be fully trained and would be drafted away. But we would be replaced by another course of trainees, who would still be training when Christmas came. Did it mean nothing to us what our successors had for Christmas dinner? Were we content that they should eat the standard navy pork, when it lay in our power to give them a real feast?

We voted to keep geese.

Some of our successors joined us later at our operational station. We asked them what they had for Christmas dinner. They said pork. They had been rather surprised, though, to receive several letters from senior officers at the Admiralty, thanking them for the geese.

Years later, after the war was over, I met a girl who had been on that course after us. She told me that on arrival they were each handed a paper on which were typed a number of subjects such as:

Basketwork
Goats
Hockey
Horses
Hens (etc.)

And were asked to tick any subject in which they were interested. On a rather foolish impulse she had ticked 'goats', and then found herself appointed Wren goatherd. She hated the goats, and they hated her, and kicked her whenever she went near them. She milked them as best she could, but as neither she nor the other Wren goatherd knew anything about either goats or milking, they soon went dry. Those who had ticked 'horses' groomed the pony and trap for church parades.

Among the dozen 'old' Wrens at the start of our course were three others from Plymouth, and though we did not know one another, the *HMS Drake* on our hat ribbons served as a swift introduction. We extended our circle to include a girl labelled *HMS Raleigh*, as *Raleigh* was also Plymouth Command. *Raleigh* was the seamanship and gunnery school for the West Country, and the sailors who had marched with us in the Warship Week parades usually came either from *Raleigh* or from *HMS Impregnable*, the West Country signal school. It was a bit embarrassing for Wrens to have to wear that particular ribbon.

At first I missed my Devonport friends desperately. Later, like other service people, I learned to form superficial friendships very quickly. It was impossible to keep up with all one's friends by letter, and genuinely friendly happy relationships dissolved for ever when drafting caused a separation. Used to schoolgirl loyalties, the apparent shallowness of this approach to human relationships worried me at first, but I learnt to accept it. The world must be strewn with people I briefly knew and liked. One runs into them unexpectedly in train carriages and restaurants. Seven years after the war I found one next to me on the *Queen Elizabeth*, bound for New York; another turned up in the United

Nations building in Geneva, and a third on a ski slope in Canada. But so began, when drafting permitted, a raft of acquaintances destined to ripen into friendships that were to endure through time and space, not just across a lifetime but across continents, as post-war marriages and careers scattered us from Canada to the Antipodes.

It would be cosy to say that we were drawn from all walks of life, but in fact we were not. Almost all of us were middle-class girls who had had a reasonably good secondary school education. At a time when it was not routine for a girl to go into higher education, a number of my telegraphist acquaintances went on to university after the war, including several to Oxford and Cambridge. Post-war careers were to speak for the range of talent assembled, for among those with whom I was to become acquainted were to be published authors and poets, the writer of a highly successful children's TV series, and women whose work was to earn them a place on the Honours' List. For those who devoted themselves to domesticity, there were several professors' wives, and some who ended with titles when their husbands rose to the top of their professions and became knights or barons.

But that was for the future. In 1942 our ages ranged from seventeen to about twenty-seven, the great majority being about twenty to twenty-two. When, after two weeks, the new recruits went into uniform, we soon forgot who was an 'old' Wren, and who was 'new', and became one homogeneous and happy bunch.

Uniform did surprisingly little to blunt the distinctive personalities of those girls. There was Gay, for instance, seventeen years old and the daughter of a Yorkshire clergyman; she was as exuberant as her name, a slim, striking girl with vivid dark eyes and a devastating talent for mimicry. She had arrived at the training depot with a bad conscience, as she had claimed, in her application to join the WRNS, that she knew Morse, which was an exaggeration, as she only knew up to D. She was busy trying to learn the rest of the alphabet, when she discovered that most of the others did not even know that much. Joy, instead of being straight from school, had worked briefly in a bank before joining up, so we regarded her as something of an authority on Life, and sought her advice on such problems as whether we should, or should not, kiss our boy-friends goodnight—a position of trust which she discharged with typical gentle humour. (Her advice, by the way, was Yes, if they asked us out more than four times, which would be proof enough that they really liked us, and were not just Out for What They Could Get.)

There was Rachel, another clergyman's daughter, smoking cigarettes through a holder, and practising a cool sophistication which went well with her brunette beauty, but kept being dissolved by gales of merriment when something tickled her sense of humour. Beryl, auburn-haired and sturdy, a grin always lurking on her shrewd face, was one of the most competent girls there, unruffled no matter what the emergency. There was Sheila, tall and guileless, with an even, generous temperament that made her one of the most reliable of friends and companions. There was Babs, with her vehement expressions and her talented fingers coaxing amazing music from the piano in the fo'c's'le; Doris, a little older than we were, a quiet girl with wide, mild blue eyes and the, to us, fascinating habit of putting mascara on her eyelashes; Titch, the former Sea Ranger, amusing us all at camp concerts; Bobbie who could rumba so beautifully.

And there were Ruin and Havoc. They were Wrens of many months, if not years, service, and we regarded them as our two special Old Salts. Ruin was a large girl, who had about her an air of former grandeur, but, like an ancient monument, everything was crumbling. Her coat did not fit, her tie was never straight, her long hair tumbled from under her hat. When she smiled her whole large face crumpled with kindness. She was much loved. Havoc's life had been one long battle against adversity, from the days when her grandmother, her only relative, had first sent her to earn her living as a domestic servant, to the time when she joined the

WRNS as a cook. By sheer persistence and native intelligence, she had fought her way into the telegraphist training school. Something of her struggle showed in her face. Where Ruin steamed, a great, if battered, capital ship, Havoc escorted with the deadly determination of a destroyer. It was after meeting Havoc that we learned to refer to our Wren hats as 'titfers', though it was some time before I knew why. 'Tit-for-tat' ... I had had my first lesson in cockney rhyming slang.

One thing rankled with me. The new entries were given official numbers in the 25,000 range. Mine, though I had already been four months in the Navy, was over 30,000, suggesting I was of a more recent vintage. The explanation was that the numbers were allocated in blocks, and the block allocated to the Plymouth Command was of higher numbers than the block allocated to the Portsmouth Command, in which jurisdiction we now were. I never quite got over it.

As there were so many new entries, we had to have gas lectures all over again. Poison gas, poison gas, poison gas — we were never allowed to forget about it for long. We wore our service gas masks while practice gas bombs were let off under our noses, so that we could learn by personal experience that the masks worked. A Petty Officer from Portsmouth came — it always seemed to be Petty Officers who were detailed for that job.

"In a gas attack," he said, "what will probably 'appen is you'll get a whiff of gas before you've 'ad time to get your mask on. And in that case, what will 'appen is you'll be sick. Vomit, see. Well, you've *not got to take your mask off*. And the next thing is this. If you don't do something about it, you're going to suffocate, see. Suffocate in your own vomit."

He looked round. We were all looking distressed, which pleased him. He took a deep breath and launched his bomb shell.

"In order not to suffocate in your own vomit, you must eat it."

He achieved the desired effect. We became very distressed.

"Why not?" he asked triumphantly. "Dogs do. If dogs do, so can you."

I've not, since that day, greatly liked dogs.

The thought of poison gas preoccupied us. At any minute we expected to see the poisonous cloud come drifting through the trees, where the yellow gas-detection plaques, programmed to turn green in the presence of gas, had been nailed up. Churchill broadcast that if the Nazis used gas we should retaliate, and then a rumour went round the Wrennery that poison gas had been used by the Nazis on the Russian front, so we felt it was only a matter of time. I became so frightened that I volunteered for the Decontamination Squad, hoping that extra knowledge would cope with my fears.

We were now *HMS Victory*, because we were an offshoot of Portsmouth. But gold tally bands were no longer obtainable, and ship names were now forbidden for security reasons, so the new entries had nothing but a simple *HMS* in yellow silk. (For similar economy reasons, R.N. officers' stripes, though still of gold braid, were applied only to the outside of the cuff, and no longer circled the whole sleeve.) We stuck to our old tally bands as long as we could, but finally we were ordered to bring ourselves up-to-date and wear the simple *HMS*. From then on we searched the shops for an *HMS* made of gold wire instead of the plain silk, but they were unobtainable.

We never really abandoned the search for gold wire tally bands. Some time later, when I was on leave in Edinburgh, I noticed a naval outfitters called Gieves in Prince's Street — suppliers of cocked hats and epaulettes for admirals, captains' silk-lined cloaks, and, I presumed, anything else the Navy might require. I went in.

A dignified elderly man dressed in a tail coat came to serve me.

"Have you any gold wire tally bands?" I asked.

He looked troubled, and inclined his head towards me. "I beg your pardon?" he said.

"Tally bands", I repeated. "Gold wire. With *HMS* on them."

He went away, the troubled expression still on his face, and fetched another assistant, as dignified as himself, but slightly younger, and to him I repeated my request. He, too, looked puzzled.

They retreated a few feet from me and held a whispered conversation, after which the elder of the two returned and said:

"Is this — er — an article of officers' apparel?"

"Oh no," I said, "Seamen have them. And Wrens."

Their worried features relaxed.

"I suggest, Madam," he said, "that you try some of the shops in the vicinity of the docks. I'm sure they will be able to help you."

So I went along the road to Leith where the little shops were full of badges, buttons and insignia for those who were not expected to do their shopping in Prince's Street, but I never managed to acquire a gold wire tally band.

A beautiful summer blazed across Hampshire. Although we were stationed in the heart of the country, travel was easy. One just went and stood in the road, and someone gave a lift. Wherever we went, our service gas masks had to go too, but as we had no 'pochettes' in those days (they were not issued until two years later) this was quite convenient, as we could cram handkerchiefs, cosmetics, and all the other paraphernalia that normally live in a handbag, into the mask. Later, when the gas scare had worn off somewhat, but the carrying of masks was still obligatory, we used to leave the mask itself in our beds, and fill the case with pyjamas, tooth brushes and anything else we wanted to take with us for a forty-eight-hour pass.

We had not the money for train fares, so hitch-hiking was essential. Sometimes commercial lorries hauled us aboard, but usually it was the Army. The Portsmouth Road was our route to London, past the scaffolding and red brick where the new Guildford Cathedral was beginning take shape, and this led us through territory occupied by the Fifth Canadian Armoured Division. The troopers of Lord Strathcona's Horse became our most trusted chauffeurs, so much so that on some occasions they would turn up at the Wrennery doors ready to escort us, though it was miles off their proper route. We felt pangs of conscience about the petrol unlawfully consumed, but they did not. Finally our CO sent for us, and said that she could not believe our soldier friends' duties led so conveniently and so consistently past the Wrennery and would we please arrange to meet them on their proper route.

But they did not seem to have a proper route. Once we went to Winchester with them. We had planned an evening of canteens and dancing, but the trooper at the wheel was dissatisfied with all the parking places. Finally he insisted on taking the truck inside the KRRC barracks, where there was an armed guard on the gate. "I don't want to leave the thing about in the streets," he explained to us later, "we're really on an exercise, and this truck's loaded with ammunition."

When the Strathconas moved away, other friendly drivers took their place. Once I rode in the cabin of a ramshackle Army lorry, driven by a well-spoken soldier in a peculiar array of clothing. Outside London we turned into his camp, where I found the rest of his regiment wearing turbans. They were Sikhs. He told me we had to abandon the lorry, but if I would wait we could continue our journey in another transport. He came out again looking extremely smart and wearing a major's uniform, a driver appeared with an immaculate car, and we were driven to the War Office in Whitehall. The major got out and said to the driver, "Take this young lady home".

But such luck was rare. Usually we got lifts to within the radius of the London underground, and then went by tube.

Sometimes one met cranks. A lorry driver with mild religious mania once spent a whole journey trying to convert me. I told him I was converted already, but it did not help. He continued to shower me with sermons and tracts which he suggested I should read and then leave about in useful places. He himself had been converted by finding a tract in a telephone booth at a particularly critical moment in his life. When I got out of the lorry, my pockets bulging with tracts, I thanked him, as I always thanked the people who drove me about.

"A lot of people thank me when they get out of this lorry," he said, "but it's not for the ride they're giving thanks."

The few civilians who had petrol and were on the move were always generous with the space in their cars. On one occasion I thumbed a car which I recognized as one that I had been in about a month previously. The driver did not recognize me, but I remembered our previous conversation.

"How's your son?" I asked him, "The one who's an instructor at Rosyth?"

"Very well", he said guardedly. "Yes, he's very well."

We drove a little further.

"Taken your yacht out yet this year?" I asked.

The car seemed to give a slight leap forward, and then settle again. The driver looked at me nervously, as if he expected to find a witch on the seat beside him. I reassured him that he'd given me a lift before.

More often than not hitch-hiking was faster, more direct and more reliable than public transport. But at first I had not liked to risk returning from a forty-eight-hour leave except by recognized transport. At the end of one such leave I had to return from a village outside Salisbury, a direct distance of about thirty-five miles. Buses into Salisbury, where I had to catch the train, were always too full on a Sunday afternoon to hold any more passengers, so first it was necessary to take a bus in the opposite direction, and get on the Salisbury bus further towards the start of the route. Thus I reached Salisbury in time to catch the Southampton train, but there was an air-raid over Southampton, our train was delayed, and by the time we got in my connection had left. After a long wait another train took me to Fareham, but by then the last bus had left Fareham. It was almost dark, and I had still twelve miles to go. There was nothing for it but to start walking.

After a mile or so I heard a car coming out of the night behind me. In my dark uniform I was practically invisible, but I waved a white handkerchief and the driver stopped. He was not going to the village where we were stationed, but passing fairly near on another road, so he told me to get in and he would drop me at the nearest point.

We then drove along roads I did not recognize until he dropped me at a road junction I had never seen before, and pointed out my route. I started along the road, which seemed to be climbing to the crest of a ridge of hills. I was carrying a large brown paper parcel containing my summer pyjamas and underclothes which I had gone home to fetch. Occasionally the moon shone, but thin clouds were streaking rapidly across it, gradually blotting out the stars. A fitful rain began, and my parcel began to disintegrate.

At last I reached the top of the hill. There in the moon-light lay an empty heath, with a few wet gorse bushes crouched by the roadside. In the centre of the heath five small roads met. I had no idea which to take, and there were no signposts, all of which had been removed in order to confuse possible invaders. The brown paper at one end of my parcel dissolved, and my summer pyjamas slid gently to the road. Rain dripped steadily from my hat. It seemed to me that one of the gorse bushes moved, and then froze again as soon as I looked straight at it. I was frightened, and wished I had someone with me.

Somewhere in the valley far away a church clock chimed. I had been seven hours trying to cover thirty-five miles. My leave pass had expired, and I was 'adrift', i.e. absent without permission. When—or if—I finally reached the Wrennery, I should be a 'defaulter'.

I stood in the rain and tried to visualize where this ridge must be in relation to the Wrennery. I remembered a line of high ground to the west of the Wrennery. Probably that was where I now stood, so if I went east I might come to country that I knew. But I did not know which of the five roads pointed east, and it was too dark to see which led downhill.

The clouds cleared for a minute, and I saw the Plough and the North Star. That gave me my direction; I chose my road and started along it. Suddenly I came on houses. All were in darkness—not only because of the black-out, but because everyone had gone to bed. I woke the occupants of one house and asked them where I was. I was within two miles of my destination.

My cabin mates were sitting up in bed waiting for me. When I came in, tired, wet and miserable, they all leapt out of bed with offers to make me hot drinks and fill hot water bottles. From that day I ceased mourning my Devonport friends. I had got new ones.

So it really seemed best not to risk delay by travelling by public transport. We continued to hitch-hike. Kind old ladies shared their picnic gooseberry tarts with us; kind old gentlemen bought us ginger beer and chips. Sometimes they would be planning to return by the same route, and would arrange to pick us up again on their way back. Only once did I ever hear of an unpleasant incident, and that was when one of our Chief Wren instructors asked to be put down at a certain spot, but the driver went past it with what she took to be evil intent. She reached for the handbrake, slammed it on, and got out of the car.

More often than not our destination was London. There were the concerts at the National Gallery, and a young, auburn-haired corporal in the RAF called Dennis Matthews who really could play the piano. Ballet was popular, but the seats were expensive and hard to get. Rachel and I hitched to London in a fish manure lorry with tickets for the eighth row of the stalls in our pockets—we had become friends once I got over my chagrin that her official number was 6,000 earlier than mine. In London it looked like rain, and we desperately hit one another to make sure the dry fish manure powder was out of our clothes before the rain began — we smelt terrible anyway.

Tickets for the ballet had cost us all our money, and when the rain began we could not go to a cinema or a restaurant in order to avoid it. If only there were a Forces canteen nearby! Suddenly I remembered something.

"I read in *The Times*", I said, "that the Athenaeum is being opened to Service people."

Probably the habitués of the Athenaeum had been evacuated, and it was now a Forces Canteen. We decided to go along. Unfortunately we were not sure which of the august buildings housed the Athenaeum, but standing on the corner of Pall Mall was a young War Reserve constable, the soft summer rain filtering in rivulets down his short rain-proof cape, and we decided to consult him.

"Please," I said, "can you tell us the way to the Athenaeum?"

He surveyed us for a moment. We were a bedraggled couple, and a faint steam was now rising from the remaining impregnation of fish manure.

"And what", he asked, "would you two be doing with the Athenaeum?"

"I read that it's now a Forces Canteen", I said.

He said that he did not think it was. In fact, he said, he was really pretty sure that we were mistaken. He did not advise us to go to the Athenaeum. So we went to Tottenham Court Road instead, bought cherries from a barrow-boy, and filled in the time till the ballet by spitting cherry stones into half the gutters in the West End.

And then the ballet! Glowing red plush seats, white brilliance on the stage, the beauty of the dancers, light and smooth and swift as sea-birds. Was it the same world in which we clumped through squad drill in our rough serge suits and our black lace-up shoes? Beryl Grey, Margot

Fonteyn, Robert Helpmann ... *Comus, Hamlet, Les Sylphides* ... for an enraptured hour or two we lived transported.

The ballet was not then at Covent Garden, but we went to Covent Garden too. The stalls had been boarded over, two dance bands were installed on a revolving platform where the stage had been, and it was the dimmest lit, slushiest, plushiest dance hall in London. It was full of the sort or flashy girls whom we contemptuously dismissed as 'civvies', and the sort of flashy men who liked them that way. What was commonly believed about Service girls' morals was precisely mirrored in what we thought of civilian girls' morals—we were always convinced that they had not joined up because they were so immoral that the Services would not have them.

Portsmouth beckoned us, being Wrens. Within a week of our arrival in bucolic surroundings, I was pining for the Hoe and the ships and the sea. Gay and I hitched to the outskirts of Portsmouth, and, finding two sailors, asked them where the sea was. They said they did not know, they had never seen it. Perhaps they were just being security-minded. We found it, and gazed at the dreaded Whale Island, *HMS Excellent*, where lurked the fiercest gunnery instructors, and models for Players cigarette packets.

Next time we returned to Pompey it was to bludgeon our way past the dockyard police and onto Nelson's *Victory*. I had forgotten my identity papers, i.e. my paybook, but was hurriedly allowed in when I began to take off my clothes in an effort to find the official identity disc, strung round my neck (worn by all Service people—it gave one's religion in the event of one becoming a casualty).

Sometimes we only went as far as the nearby villages for dances in the local canteens. The Hampshire countryside was peppered with Army and Navy units, and every village seemed to have its Forces Canteen, run by the YMCA, the Salvation Army, or the NAAFI.

For it must be admitted that, while we were all very keen to Win the War, we had a second purpose not very deeply buried, and that was to Find Romance. With this in mind, we persuaded our officers to allow us sufficient money from the Mess funds to hold a dance. We invited about a hundred sailors from *HMS Collingwood*, the naval training base at Fareham.

It was a flop. The sailors were fairly tough Seamen and Gunners, and they thought us la-di-da and toffy-nosed. We thought them not very well brought up, and furthermore many of them had not been in the Navy long enough to learn to keep their fingernails clean. Most of them left the dance quite early and went to the local pubs to play darts, ping-pong, even the gramophone, anything rather than socialize with these snooty, posh-spoken suburban girls. We went short of dancing partners. Nevertheless, a large, rather sweaty stoker taught me to rumba, for which I am eternally in his debt.

But there was also at the dance a tall handsome Army officer. He danced all the time with a girl called Pat, and it looked as if there was at any rate one budding romance. Pat was on the Duty Watch, and was due to wash up, but aided and abetted by a sentimental Wren officer there was some hurried back-room reorganization of the duty roster so that Pat would not have to wash up and the course of true love could be permitted to run smooth.

It was all to no avail. Pat was not at all interested in the Army officer, and didn't care whether she ever saw him again. The initiative was not futile, however, as he was hurriedly snapped up by a Wren called Dorothy, who never let anything good go to waste.

Dorothy knew what she wanted, and shocked some of the girls from Wimbledon and Harrow. She also knew what she didn't want, and to prove it she once emptied a glass of lemonade on a soldier's head. The girls from Wimbledon and Harrow were even more shocked.

We all loved to dance. Many of us were still in our teens, and we had an immense amount of surplus energy. If there was no dancing anywhere near, we danced reels and eightsomes in the Wrennery. Sometimes we pushed one another over on the soft grass and fought in a friendly way out of sheer excess of energy.

How we were ever going to sit still on watch we did not know. For our main task, after all, was to learn to be watch-keeping telegraphists.

Chapter IV

The U-Boat Winter

Every day we ditted and dahed. Visualizing Morse as a series of dots and dashes was rapidly eliminated from our minds; speed depended on our capacity to achieve a completely automatic connection between what we heard and what we wrote down. The connection between ear and hand had to become so automatic that we ceased to use the conscious part of our minds. I remember a moment of panic when I completely forgot what the symbol 'dit dah' meant, and while I struggled to remember, I watched with interest as my own hand reacted to the stimulus by writing—quite correctly—the letter 'A'.

Our instructors were Chief Wren telegraphists. Very soon every sound we heard seemed to be in Morse. The birds sang in Morse code. Dah dit dit dah dah dah went the thrush. The pump pumped water in Morse, the trees, swaying in the wind, sent out Morse messages in the creaking of their limbs.

There were others who, like me, had learnt the Morse code before they came on the course. We made swift progress. Within three weeks we were just managing to read at nineteen words per minute, and our instructors were so pleased with us they began calling us by our Christian names. Speeds were climbing. Twenty-two wpm, twenty-six (which was passing-out speed, so we were up to scratch), finally a brief burst at thirty!* Ever and anon a commander from the Admiralty came to check our progress. He sent for me.

"I see", he said, "that during yesterday's transmissions you made eleven errors. How did that happen? It won't do. The Navy requires 100% percent accuracy. You must do better."

Soon our progress was being impeded not by the speed at which we could read Morse, but the speed at which we could write. Dictation classes were held, at which the sole object was to write faster and faster and faster (a skill for which, at college after the war, I was immensely grateful). Senior officers from the Admiralty would appear from time to time and walk round behind our chairs investigating our hand-writing through a magnifying glass.

There was a puzzling feature of this training, which we discussed with surprise among ourselves. We were never shown how to transmit, or offered the opportunity to practise. On May 13th, about a month after our training began, we signed the Official Secrets Act. Sometime over the following fortnight we were let into the terrible secret. We were not ordinary telegraphists, we were Y-Branch, Special Operator Intercept Telegraphists,* snooping on enemy ships and naval signals traffic. Not only would we be recording enemy messages for decoding purposes, above all we would be scouring the airwaves for transmissions from enemy ships, especially the U-boats, so that their position could be determined by HF/DF (high frequency direction finding) and they could be sunk.

It was a shock and an unpleasant one. Vaguely, when I applied to be a telegraphist, I saw myself as a sort of '999' telephone operator, taking pleas for help and sending ships

---

* For those in the know, these speeds will seem very high. The explanation is that we counted only four digits to the word, not the usual five. The German naval enigma code was transmitted in four digit groups — not that we knew that, at this early stage of our training.

* Colloquially abbreviated to 'Tels (SO)'

and aircraft to the rescue. Instead, I was to listen to some German sailor and then do my best to get him killed. I felt no animosity whatever towards German sailors, with their blue eyes and caps with (unlike the British) ribbons hanging down the back. And girl-friends at home in Hamburg and Bremen. I felt as if I had just been appointed a member of an execution squad.

Today, seventy-odd years later, with women bearing arms practically on the front line, my reaction must seem incomprehensible. But I came of a generation which still saw women as primarily nurturers, not destroyers. Patriotic, of course, but in the Nurse Cavell mode.

I sat on my bunk in 'Hardy' cabin, with its neat rows of blue and white counterpanes, all carefully spread so that the anchor in the centre pointed with the flukes towards the foot of the bunk. Opposite me, on her bunk, sat Rachel.

"But you *are* saving British sailors", said Rachel. "Every time you get German sailors killed, you save British lives."

"I don't want to do this job", I said.

"Somebody's got to do it", said Rachel. "You can't expect other people to do all the dirty work."

I sought out one of our Chief Wren instructors, and asked if I could be transferred to the W-Branch, the non-intercept telegraphists. She was astonished. "This is a marvellous job", she said. She held out no hope whatever of a transfer.

All my zeal evaporated, and for several days my work suffered. Then something happened that changed everything. On the June 25th 1942 *The Daily Telegraph* published an account of events in Poland, of Jewish men and boys being made to dig trenches, and stand beside them to be shot, of children in orphanages and women being butchered, even of sealed vans loaded with Jews being pumped full of lethal gas. It was beyond belief. Of course we knew the Jews were suffering gross injustice, discrimination, confiscation of property, public humiliation, unjustified incarceration in 'labour' camps (as we thought they were)—even, occasionally, street violence. Two hundred Jewish boys had in fact sheltered in our school over the Christmas holidays of 1938, refugees after Krystallnacht. Despicable though the persecution was, it had no more moved the British people to call for war than did Idi Amin's later persecution of the Uganda Asians (though revulsion at Nazi conduct fuelled the flames of support when war came for other reasons). What was portrayed in that *Telegraph* article was no longer persecution—it was systematic extermination. We know now that this had been going on for many months, but it was not then public knowledge, and *The Telegraph*'s was the first newsroom to risk publishing what others had been dismissing as black propaganda.

I was reconciled to my job. It had to be stopped, no matter what the cost.

Telegraphists read (and transmit) coded messages of whose content they are ignorant. But there is another set of codes which they must understand, the codes which constitute the so called 'operators' chat' in which operators discuss such matters as signal strength, transmitting intentions, etc. There is an international 'Q' code, such as 'QTC: I have a message for you', 'I am changing frequency', etc., and a raft of simple letter codes, such as 'CQ: Calling all Ships', 'R: I am receiving you', many of which can be turned into a question by adding 'IMI' ('R IMI—Are you receiving me?'). Though we would only be eavesdroppers, these we now had to start learning. Much, though not all, of the German Navy's 'operators' chat' used the international Q code, but we had to tackle also the Italian (and, much later in our naval careers, the Japanese) operators' codes. We were no longer allowed to retain overnight possession of our notebooks, which were removed every evening for safekeeping. It was probably in reference to this phase of our training that, in mid-June, my diary, guardedly and rightly non-specific, notes a 'terrific row for not being careful enough with secret stuff. No more warnings—next time a report is to be made that we're not fit to be W/T operators'. By now there was talk of our future postings, Scarborough for the Germans;

Flowerdown, outside Winchester, for the Italians. In my diary these options I (perhaps rather fatuously) concealed from casual prying eyes by using the Greek alphabet, though in fact security rested not in concealing locations but by total silence on the subject of what went on there. They were simply 'RN Shore Wireless' stations.

There were other challenges. We had to learn to operate the Navy's high-frequency wireless equipment, the redoubtable, reliable American HRO. It was no longer a question of a buzzer on the table, we had to learn to find a signal among the myriad noises on the radio waves; to read it though thunder storms caused electrical disturbances that almost split our ear-drums open; to read it though unidentifiable stations broadcasting dance music in Latin America all but swamped us; to read it though it might be the merest tremble of the ether, the fading signal from a sinking ship whose batteries were dying.

We studied the theory of wireless transmission, the significance of the beat frequency oscillator, the mathematical relationship between cycles and wavelengths, the low and medium frequencies which would bounce back off the atmospheric layers all round the world, and the VHF, very high frequencies, which exited straight through the layers, so could only be used within the direct (eye-line) vicinity of the transmitter (though sometimes freak conditions would interrupt the departure of VHF circuits, and we would suddenly pick up, for instance, Chicago taxi drivers whose local chat was being bounced unexpectedly back to earth). Our evening browsing of the sets could take us anywhere, Istanbul, Ankara … boundaries melted away.

We went to extra evening classes. The Nazis were within hailing distance of Alexandria. The wireless in the fo'c's'le played *Deep in the Heart of Texas*. We could read at thirty wpm. As soon as quarters were available for us at the RN Shore Wireless stations, we could pass out.

And then, on September 3rd 1942, the anniversary of the outbreak of the war, twenty of us were told that we had qualified as telegraphists. Until our course trained, all Wren Telegraphist Special Operators were automatically rated Chief Wren, but with the expansion of the branch, this policy came to an end, and we were the unlucky ones who were the first to go on the job as Ordinary Wrens. We were issued with sparkers' badges — wings with a lightning flash through the centre. Lovingly we fitted little pieces of cotton wool behind the wings so that they would stand up in relief from the background of the badge. On the right arm, half way between the shoulder seam and the elbow, we sewed the badges on, and went home on leave.

No Air Force pilot was ever prouder of his wings.

A fortnight later, we were on the job, in Scarborough.

"You know what they are, don't you", said assured voices, not bothering to conceal the fact that they were talking about us. "They're *French* Wrens."

We had paused in London to turn in our pudding-bowl hats and be issued with the jaunty little sailor caps which had just been approved for Wrens. These little round hats were being issued in the main ports and the districts where concentrations of Wrens were heaviest, but were only gradually lapping out across the countryside. By the time we reached York we had become a sensation. Heads turned and eyes followed us wherever we went.

Scarborough too was intrigued by the new uniforms, and it was some days before the less mature section of the population stopped shouting "Ship Ahoy!" and "The Fleet's in!" whenever we appeared in the streets. Some of the children cheekily applied to us the old maxim 'Touch a sailor's collar for luck', and we found ourselves surrounded by shrill children leaping into the air in an effort to touch the small neat serge collars at the back of our jackets.

We were billeted in the Hotel Cecil, a pleasant building which the following spring was to be redolent with the wonderful smell of the wallflowers that carpeted its approach.

Work began in earnest. Our journey from the Cecil to our wireless station was made by lorry, an open truck with a back hatch that swung down, up which we hauled one another, rickety benches down either side, and a canvas awning attached to metal staves onto which clung those who had not got on in time to sit on a bench. We were sheltered from the rain, but not from the cold, which grew more intense as the winter progressed, and we were grateful to be handed scarves and pullovers labelled 'Canadian Red Cross' and the Province of origin. Mine said 'Province of Alberta'. I wondered if the knitter would have been disappointed to learn that her efforts ended up not at sea but on women ashore, but we were deeply grateful for them. Even so, we often ended the bumpy ride stiff with cold for the start of a winter Middle watch.

Already while training we had been assigned to watches, but now we were working full naval watches. Weekends disappeared. Every hour had to be covered. Sailors worked in three watches, a fifty-six hour week (average eight hours a day), we in four, i.e. a forty-two hour week (average six hours a day), so we could hardly complain that our pay was far lower than the matelots. With full qualification we had now progressed to 16s 4d a week (81 post-decimal pennies). But of course we did not in fact work six hours a day. The four-watch system had us on Day One working a Forenoon watch, 0800 to 1300, then off all afternoon (sleep) till 2300 when we returned to do the Middle and Morning watches, 2300 to 0800. We had Day Two off to sleep, and returned on Day Three from 1300 to 2300, which we called the First, though strictly speaking it covered most of the Afternoon and both Dog Watches, as well as the First. The fourth day was a Stand Off, when we could do as we liked before returning, on Day Five, to the difficult fourteen hours of Day One that we called our 'Waterloo'. The sailors didn't get a stand-off, and I wasn't sorry to be regarded as a feeble woman. It was not too onerous a routine.

We had to acquire a new rhythm of eating and sleeping. Night watches meant work—they were not a token appearance with half of us in some rest room snoozing. We had to be alert the whole time. This was almost impossible unless one could get some sleep during the afternoon, but it was some time before we could accustom ourselves to dropping off to sleep at will in the middle of the day. No one thought of sleeping pills, but we canvassed many psychological methods of inducing sleep when one was not in the least sleepy.

"Let your mind go blank."

"Pretend you're surrounded by black velvet, nothing anywhere but oceans of black velvet."

"Relax until you feel you will drop right through the mattress."

"Make sure your feet are warm. You can't sleep if your feet are cold."

"Pretend you are thistledown, and just float away."

In the end, most of us acquired a facility for dropping asleep whenever we wanted to. Sleeping when we came off night watch was less difficult, as one was so tired, but when we started on the job we were at first tormented by imaginary Morse signals in our head which persisted for an hour or two after we came off a long watch.

A few girls never did acquire the ability to sleep during the day. Six months later we tried a new system, a week on night duty followed by three weeks of working the day watches, as it was thought that it might make it easier to work at night and sleep during the day if we did it for seven consecutive nights and days. At this stage the few girls who could not learn to sleep in the day had to change to other branches which did not keep watches.

None of us managed our first night watch very successfully. We had tried to sleep before it, but woke from our dozing feeling sick. At about half past ten at night we clambered into the back of our open lorry. At the door of the wireless station, at that time a small cottage out in the

Yorkshire countryside (later to be exchanged, under the exigencies of war, for a large purpose-built underground establishment), we fell back a pace—the air was foul, and growing fouler every minute, from the smoke of the reeking pipes favoured by the retired seadogs with whom we worked, supplemented by the (cheap rate) cigarettes favoured by the matelots. Nine hours doubled up all night over our wireless sets in that atmosphere gave us cramp in the stomach, and when the Forenoon watch relieved us at 8 o'clock the next morning we were hollow-eyed, grey faced and weak at the knees. We shuffled back to our Quarters, but could not face breakfast. Within days we had adjusted ourselves to everything except the tobacco, and were relatively bright-eyed, and certainly hungry when we came off watch in the morning.

We sustained ourselves through the night with sandwiches, the components for which were left in the Mess for us to make up our own; usually beetroot and National Loaf, sometimes rather strong mousetrap cheese. Cups of tea were brought round, though there were times, in that winter of 1942/3, when the pressure of work was such that there wasn't time to drink them. Of course no headphones could be unmanned for a moment, and any departure to answer a call of nature had to be covered by a relief operator when one was available—sometimes entailing a wait of as long as two hours. We would go off watch so exhausted that we would crawl into our bunks without even stopping to put curlers in our hair, which, according to the women's magazines in the fo'c's'le, was a sluttish thing to do.

As for the work, now we were really exposed to the cacophony of the airwaves. We were, after all, interlopers, the transmissions were not designed for our ears, and sometimes we had to pursue our signals through dance bands and myriad other irrelevant signals. Great concentration and very good hearing were required, hearing that had to suffer the assaults of sudden violent electric storms crashing on our headphones. It did not seem to damage our hearing, which on the whole seemed to become almost painfully acute, and remained so until old age imposed its inevitable blunting. Even now I find loud noises unpleasant, and it left a permanent inhibition on my capacity to enjoy loud music, e.g. organs.

We did not know whether the decoders, whoever and wherever they were, were managing to decode the messages we so laboriously took down. Sometimes, when the seasons affected the famous layers in the sky, and a mass change of frequency took place, our charge-hands would suggest approximate ranges where we'd be well advised to search for our stations; often we had latched onto our 'control' (the German transmitters were very distinctive) before all the associated German sub-stations had tuned in, which was satisfying. It occurred to me to wonder whether our charge-hands had had some sort of external hint, but I never asked. 'Need to know', was the ever-guiding principle. If you didn't need to know, you didn't ask.

The truth is, we weren't all that interested in the decoding aspect of our job. Finding enemy ships, above all U-boats, that's where we saw our usefulness lying. Those of us on the four main U-boat frequencies were desperate not to miss a transmission from a U-boat. All ship transmissions were rare and as brief as possible—radio silence was the rule. At its briefest, a U-boat message could be as little as eleven digits, though most were a bit more than that. We had to shout the number of the frequency we were on, which would be immediately repeated by the charge-hand at an elevated desk in the middle of the room into a microphone on his desk connected to all the D/F (direction finding) stations from end to end of the country. They had to tune in to the transmission and get a bearing. This they reported to our control, and ... Well, what then? Our understanding was that these details then went to the Admiralty and in particular to Admiral Sir Max Horton, C-in-C Western Approaches in Liverpool, where the information would be plotted on a great wall chart, reaching to the ceiling, tended by Wren plotters on ladders. This is the source of the story that Sir Max said either Wrens must be issued with bell-bottoms, or all future convoys must be routed south. On the basis of this information, so we understood, convoy routes would be adjusted and escort vessels warned of the imminence of attack.

A U-boat signal was recognizable because it began with a barred B, twice repeated. Barred letters were variations of the normal Morse alphabet, indicated in writing by a line over the letter. The Germans used them quite a bit, for instance in the call signs of their shore stations. (An A-Bar, for instance, was an A repeated: not dit-dah, but dit-dah-dit-dah. One shore station, LLA-Bar, thus had the rhythm dit-dah-dit-dit, dit-dah-dit-dit, dit-dah-dit-dah, which immediately brought to mind the popular song of the period, *Do you remember one September afternoon?* All this was to have renewed significance much later on, when we had to master Japanese Morse). B was dah-dit-dit-dit, B-Bar was dah-dit-dit-dit-dah. It was known as a Beer-Bar because in the early part of the war Beer was the Navy's phonetic appellation of B, and this was not changed as the phonetics were altered over time with the arrival of the Americans and with other innovations to make the phonetics more universally acceptable. Normally, the Beer-Bar itself (but not the following message) was transmitted slowly, and it seemed the most menacing sound in the world, calculated to bring any operator up in goose pimples. If, after the two Beer-Bars, a number was appended, you knew you had failed, for only the German control was allowed to assign a number to a signal, and what you were hearing was the German control's acknowledgement. That was pure humiliation. Somehow, you'd missed the chance to get a bearing. U-boat signals were rare, but at the height of the Battle of the Atlantic in March 1943, there were, in one twenty-four hours, over 100 such signals on the frequency on which I was working. Not necessarily, or even probably, 100 different U-boats of course, but 100 attempts to get a message through.

It wasn't only U-boats of course; there were also the surface raiders for which we kept anxious and on the whole unsuccessful watch. One friend of mine, listening on a frequency covering the South Atlantic, had a rare ship signal, and was later told by the charge-hand that if she never did anything else in the whole war, she had earned her keep. We were led to believe she had tracked the *Deutschland*, but, as usual, we did not really know.

And then it was Christmas, and the Wrennery—indeed, the nation as a whole, children and adults alike—was engulfed in a measles epidemic. Rachel and I had been sticking closely together. We were accommodated in double bunks in the erstwhile single rooms of the hotel, I liked top bunks, Rachel preferred bottom, so as long as we stuck together we could both have what we preferred. Just before Christmas of 1942 she was found to have measles, so she was sent to hospital, and I was quarantined by being isolated in the Sick Bay. I was wretched. I should miss all the Christmas fun and jollity.

I told the MO that I had been in quarantine for one disease after another all through my school days, and never managed to catch anything except chicken pox when I was six. Scarlet fever, measles, German measles, mumps—I had been in contact with them all, and never managed to develop any of them. I just had a natural immunity. After six days my arguments prevailed, and I was let out on Christmas Eve.

My Watch had arranged a big party for Christmas Day. Everyone came—the Signal Corps, the Royal Artillery, the Navy, the Marines, the Royal Air Force and the Hertfordshire Yeomanry. When the party was over and they had gone home we made one last festive gesture: we shared a bottle of port between about twelve of us, and drank it from our tooth-mugs.

Next day I went on watch with a pounding headache. It seemed that I had a hangover, hanging on one half toothmugful of port. I confessed as much to the girl next to me.

She looked at me closely.

"You look very funny", she said. "In fact, if you ask me, you've got measles."

She asked the girl next to her what she thought. She also thought I had measles. After that everyone put in for a relief so that they could leave their seats and come and look at me. There was general agreement that I was suffering from measles, not port. Naval transport was ordered, and the charge-hand told me several times not to worry, but just to keep warm. They had asked for a blanket to come up with the transport.

I was not worrying about measles, but about what the MO would say when he saw me. In fact he took one look at me, said "You pest!" and walked out of the room. The nursing sister of the Queen Alexandra's Royal Naval Nursing Service sent me in an ambulance to the local Pest House.

Oddly, there were virtually no adults there. There was only a corporal in the Royal Artillery who had scarlet fever, and an airman recovering from meningitis. The other measles case was a small boy of five, and he and I shared a room.

I disliked the little boy very much. He was unctuous.

"Do you know", he would say, "that you have had your bed made three times already today? I've only had my bed made once."

"You haven't drunk up your milk. I have."

He was inquisitive, too.

"Where have you been?" he would say. "Why did you get out of bed again?"

"Because they don't bring me bed-pans the way they do you", I explained testily, and let him work it out. He recovered and went home. I was glad.

Back at the Wrennery measles was spreading like purple loose-strife. There were four more cases within twenty-four hours of mine, so I felt I could not be guilty of initiating the epidemic. Nevertheless, the MO was unforgiving—or perhaps over-worked—for he did not come to see me. All the other measles cases went to other hospitals, and I felt very isolated and lonely. For several days I tried to read—no one had told me that the eyes should be rested when one has measles, and on the contrary mine were being hard-used, as I had left my glasses behind at the Wrennery. But my eyes became so sore I had to stop reading.

After a while the airman with meningitis recovered from days of delirium. The middle-aged nurse, who only came near me in order to tell me how her 'darling boy' was getting on, was delighted. He was not allowed out of bed, but no one seemed to care whether I stayed in bed or not, so I sat on the floor at the door of his room and we passed the time of day in conversation. He was rather a darling boy, but keener on the Russian Revolution than I was.

After ten days, the MO came and told me I could return to Quarters. But it must have been a very virulent measles germ, as many of us developed complications. I had never in my life been ill for more than a few days, and I was furious that any miserable little germ had got the better of me. I was off duty for two more weeks, but at the station they were short-staffed, and after that, complications or no complications, we went back on duty unless our ears were so affected that we could not read Morse. My trouble was swollen glands, which prevented me wearing my collar, as it would no longer reach round my neck, so I went back on night watch with my Province of Alberta Comfort Scarf concealing the fact that I had no collar or tie.

For the sets had to be manned. We know now, though we did not know it then, that it was in that winter of 1942–43 that Admiral Doenitz made his real bid for U-boat control of the Atlantic. From post-war revelations we know that by the end of January, as we took our measly snuffles and coughs back into the watch-room, a hundred U-boats were attacking our ships in the north and central Atlantic. Only years later did we know what was really happening out on the grey waters. Losses of allied merchant ships were so heavy that in

March 1943 the Arctic convoys to Russia were postponed, as their escorts were needed to reinforce Atlantic convoys. In mid-March came the biggest convoy battle of the whole war, when forty U-boats attacked two convoys, and sent twenty-one Allied ships to the bottom. *British Intelligence in the Second World War (Vol. II 1981)* states "The battle which was fought in the Atlantic between December 1942 and May 1943 was the most prolonged and complex battle in the history of naval warfare". The Seamen were suffering rather worse deprivations than the loss of two cups of tea and a certain amount of energy.

But all we saw or heard of it at the time was Morse, Morse, Morse. And beetroot sandwiches.

Anne's 20th birthday, 25th February 1943

PLAYER'S CIGARETTES

H.M.S. "HOOD"

PLAYER'S CIGARETTES

H.M.S. "REPULSE"

PLAYER'S CIGARETTES

H.M.S. "EXETER"

H.M.S. "HOOD." *British Battle Cruiser.* Begun under the Emergency War Programme in 1916, H.M.S. *Hood* was built by John Brown & Co., Clydebank, and cost about £6,000,000. She has a speed of 31 knots, a displacement of 42,100 tons and carries a complement of 1,341. Her armament consists of eight 15-inch guns, twelve 5.5-inch guns, four 4-inch anti-aircraft guns and subsidiary weapons, besides six 21-inch torpedo tubes. Aircraft are to be added in 1939. She is fitted with outside bulges as protection against under-water attack, and has specially thickened side armour and conning tower. The *Hood*, although over 18 years old, is still reckoned as a first-class fighting unit. (No. 4)

H.M.S. "REPULSE." *British Battle Cruiser.* "Renown" *Class.* Provided for by the 1914-15 Navy estimates, the two ships of this class were both built on the Clyde, at a cost of about £3,000,000 each. Both have been extensively reconstructed. The armament consists of six 15-inch and twelve 4-inch guns with numbers of subsidiary weapons, including 21-inch torpedo tubes. Four aircraft with catapult are in the equipment as reconstructed. The two ships each have a displacement of 32,000 tons, a speed of 28-29 knots and carry a complement of about 1,200. Owing to the additional armour protection which has been provided, the speed has been reduced from the original 31 knots. (No. 3)

H.M.S. "EXETER." *British Cruiser,* "York" *Class.* This class, numbering two ships, is a modification of the three-funnelled *Dorsetshire* type which preceded it, being 1,585 tons lighter. Originally it was intended that there should be three funnels, but the necessity of saving space decided that the two forward uptakes should be trunked into a single casing. Built at Devonport Dockyard, the *Exeter* has a displacement of 8,390 tons. Her complement is 600 and her speed 32 knots with 80,000 b.h.p. Her armament is exceptionally heavy, consisting of six 8-inch guns, with adequate subsidiary weapons, including 21-inch torpedo tubes. She carries two aircraft with catapults. (No. 6)

PLAYER'S CIGARETTES

H.M.S. "NORFOLK"

PLAYER'S CIGARETTES

H.M.S. "CURLEW"

PLAYER'S CIGARETTES

H.M.S. "SOUTHAMPTON"

sunk by bombs off coast of Norway, End of May 3/1940. 4 officers, 5 ratings lost.

H.M.S. "NORFOLK." *British Cruiser.* This design is unquestionably that of a powerful war ship, possessing fine seagoing qualities and especially useful for the protection of ocean trade, the armament being extremely powerful. Built on the Clyde, the *Norfolk* has a displacement of 9,975 tons. Her complement is 650 and her speed over 32 knots on 80,000 h.p. Her guns include eight 8-inch, eight 4-inch high-angle and twenty subsidiary weapons, with eight quadrupled tubes for 21-inch torpedoes. She has one aircraft, with catapult. This class was projected under the 1926-27 estimates, and the *Norfolk* was completed in June 1930. (No. 7)

Nr by springers in an raid on hull of Kent

H.M.S. "SOUTHAMPTON." *British Cruiser. "Southampton" Class.* This ship gives her name to one of the latest of the cruiser classes, numbering ten ship. Their displacement varies from 9,100 tons to 10,000 tons. Somewhat unusual in appearance, they are very smart and rakish-looking vessels, and were the first ships to mount 6-inch guns in triple turrets. The armament consists of twelve 6-inch guns, six forward and six aft. With a speed of 32-33 knots, their heavy volume of rapid gun-fire should render these vessels very effective fighting units. All ten ships were launched during 1936-38. The subsidiary armament includes six 21-inch tripled torpedo tubes. (No. 8)

H.M.S. "CURLEW." *British Anti-aircraft Cruiser. "Ceres" Class.* This vessel was built under the Emergency War Programme in 1916 and completed in 1917, by Vickers, as a light cruiser. This ship and the *Coventry* were reconstructed and re-armed in 1935 to fit them for the special duties of anti-aircraft vessels. Thus their armament consists of a large number of rapid fire anti-aircraft guns, including ten 4-inch guns on high-angle mountings, supported by multiple machine guns and a number of other weapons. H.M.S. *Curlew* has a speed of 29 knots on 40,000 h.p., a displacement of 4,290 tons, and carries a crew of 400. Six other vessels of similar type are to undergo conversion to anti-aircraft cruisers. (No. 9)

GERMANS MURDER 700,000 JEWS IN POLAND

TRAVELLING GAS CHAMBERS

DAILY TELEGRAPH REPORTER

More than 700,000 Polish Jews have been slaughtered by the Germans in the greatest massacre in the world's history. In addition, a system of starvation is being carried out in which the number of deaths, on the admission of the Germans themselves, bids fair to be almost as large.

The most gruesome details of mass killing, even to the use of poison gas, are revealed in a report sent secretly to Mr. S. Zygielboim, Jewish representative on the Polish National Council in London, by an active group in Poland. It is strongly felt that action should be taken to prevent Hitler from carrying out his threat that five minutes before the war ends, however it may end, he will exterminate all Jews in Europe.

It was the avowed intention of the Germans from the early days of the war to exterminate the Jewish population on Polish territory.

In a 1940 New Year message Gauleiter Greiser said that the only use to be made of the Poles was as slaves for Germany, but for the Jews there was no future. This extermination policy began in 1941 in Eastern Galicia, and everywhere the procedure has been the same.

Men and boys between 14 and 60 have been driven together into one place, usually a public square or a cemetery, and there killed, either by shooting, machine-guns or grenades. They had to dig their own graves beforehand.

HOSPITAL VICTIMS

Children in orphanages, pensioners in almshouses and the sick in hospitals have been shot. Women have been killed in the streets. In many places Jews were deported to "unknown destinations" and killed in neighbouring woods.

In Vilna 50,000 Jews were murdered in November. The total number slaughtered in this district and around Lithuanian Kovno is 300,000.

Practically all the Jews in Zyrovice, Lachovice, Mira, Kosov and other similar towns have been killed. In Rovne the murders began early in November. In three days and nights nearly 15,000 men, women and children were shot. Total deaths in other places have been:—

Lvov, 30,000	Tarnopol, 5,000
Stanislavov, 15,000	Brzezany, 4,000
Sambin, 9,000	Zloczov, 2,000
Kolomea, 5,000	

SLAUGHTER BY GAS

In November the slaughter of Jews by gas in the Polish territories incorporated in the Reich also began. A special van fitted as a gas chamber was used into which were crowded 90 victims at a time. The bodies were buried in special graves dug in the Lubardski Forest.

On an average 1,000 Jews were gassed daily. In Chelmno from November last to March 5,000 from four towns, together with 35,000 from the Lodz ghetto, and a number of gypsies, were murdered in this way.

In February the extermination of Jews started in the so-called General Government, the eastern part of which was not incorporated in the Reich. The Gestapo paid daily visits to the Jewish quarters and killed people systematically in the streets and houses.

In March 25,000 Jews were deported from Lublin in sealed wagons to an "unknown destination." All trace of them has been lost. About 3,000 more were put into barracks in a Lublin suburb. Now there is not a single Jew there.

In Cracow during March 50 men on a proscribed list were shot outside their homes. A similar number of men and women were killed outside their street doors during an arranged night of terror in the ghetto. All social groups in the ghetto were affected. More such nights are expected.

The Warsaw ghetto, actually an extensive concentration camp, houses 600,000 Jews on an average of 13 to a room. Before the war, when the district had twice as many houses, the total population was 130,000.

All children under five and all adults over 50 are refused medical supplies. This means that only a minimum of aid reaches the inside of the barrier to allay the ravages of typhus and typhoid.

According to statistics issued in Poland by the German authorities the number of funerals from the Warsaw ghetto rose from 900 in January, 1941, to 5,520 in August.

Statistics available from secret sources in Poland show that during the whole year there were no fewer than 76,000 funerals. A large proportion of the deaths were due to starvation.

In the three years 1939-1941 the number of deaths in Warsaw alone rose from 7,696 to 42,239. The Jewish population of the ghetto had risen in that time from 375,000 to 407,000 through the influx of Jews deported from other provinces and countries.

I understand that the Polish Government intends to make the facts in this report known to the British and Allied Governments.

100 AIRFIELDS IN 3 MONTHS

AUSTRALIA'S FEAT

MELBOURNE, Wednesday.

Brig.-Gen. Hugh J. Casey, Engineer Officer at Gen. MacArthur's headquarters, revealed to-day that at least 100 aerodromes had been built for the Allied Air Forces in Australia in the past three months.

"Requirements of Australia's huge construction programme," he added, "include improvement to port facilities, depots for reserve supplies, more roads and railway sidings. Because of lack of labour, plant and material, it is necessary to confine works to bare essentials."

Major-Gen. G. H. Brett, C.-in-C. Allied Air Forces in Australia, writing in the Melbourne Herald to-day, says: "We have been promised a flood of aircraft from Britain, the United States and Canada—already it is assuming massive proportions."—Reuter.

Daily Telegraph article 25th June 1942

Wartime Gibraltar

Gibraltar Harbour

Anne in tropical uniform in Gibraltar

In Gibraltar off-duty but still wearing naval issue white canvas
lace-up shoes, as none of us had any other.
Anne and Duncan on far left

Marilyn Monroe moment averted!

Anne and Duncan in Gibraltar. Duncan is in tropical uniform:
Ratings' Best Wear No. 6 Suit

With Duncan on a long-awaited visit to Algeciras, Spain

The Gibraltar draft. Back row from left: Anne, Vera ('Havoc'),
Freda G, Beryl (the singer), Evelyn, Jean, Freda L
Front row: Sheila, Beryl (the shrewd), Rachel, Doris, Mary

Return journey: Deck hockey on HMS Ravager

Demonstrating stroppiness following long wait for inspection in the
cold and damp at Signal School, 1944

THE GOVERNMENT CODE AND CYPHER SCHOOL

Anne Glyn-Jones

*The Government wishes to express
to you its deepest gratitude
for the vital service you performed
during World War II*

Gordon Brown

Rt Hon Gordon Brown MP
Prime Minister

July 2009

Chapter V

Foreign Service Beckons

Much of our off-duty time was spent searching the town for something other than beetroot to put in our sandwiches. There really was nothing. Once, my mother was able to send me a jar of Heinz Sandwich Spread from home. Delectable. Sometimes she sent me a special filler she made out of white sauce, marmite and parsley, which we thought delicious at the time, but there was not often enough margarine to spare to make the sauce. So mostly it was beetroot.

Scarborough in wartime was in some respects dismal. The beaches were mined, the cliffs thick with barbed wire, and the hotels all requisitioned for Service people. In marked contrast to Plymouth, the atmosphere was not particularly friendly to Service people. Perhaps we were resented because we filled the hotels that were their peace-time livelihood — but there would have been no summer visitors anyway, since Scarborough was classified as a 'defence area'. Whatever the reason, it seemed to us that we always had to wait in shops or cafés until every civilian had been served.

And no one asked us to their homes. Sometimes, walking along the streets late on a winter's afternoon, we would look into the cosy front parlours with fires glowing in the hearth, and would feel a wave of nostalgia for our own homes, and a wave of loathing for the fo'c's'le, the Mess and all other aspects of communal living. Once the Quakers gave a tea party for us, but otherwise we did not meet the local people.

Then one of the people who had befriended me in Plymouth heard that I was in Scarborough, and wrote to someone she knew in a nearby village. I was asked to tea in a lovely house standing above the sea, with bright fragrant flower beds tumbling to the cliff's edge.

My hostess had a little boy of two, and another child was well on the way. Both she and the boy were two of the most beautiful human beings I had ever seen. I played in the nursery with the little boy, and tried to talk to the mother, but she seemed only to half-hear what I said, and her eyes, when she looked at me, were far away.

She had a friend there, and the friend told me that the boy's father was at sea, and letters from him were long overdue.

"I don't suppose it means anything", I said. "Mail often gets held up."

But the beautiful wife was right. Notification that her husband was lost at sea arrived two weeks later. He never came home to the house at the sea's edge, and the new baby was born without a father.

As a Service community, Scarborough was busy. We no longer had to hitch from canteen to canteen across the countryside for our entertainment. Canteen-crawls, a favourite pastime of ours, could be accomplished on foot. Two or three local dance halls held dances every night of the week, and we could dance to our heart's content. Besides our own sailors, there were Royal Marines in Scarborough, three Initial Training Wings for RAF Air Crew, and units of the Herts and Essex Yeomanries, the Green Howards, the South Wales Borderers, the Guards Armoured Division, the Signals, and the RASC. We never lacked dancing partners.

No one had told us about the sex-war. Self-respect we may have had, but not pride. It had not yet dawned on us that men were exploitable. If the air cadets offered to buy us a drink we usually said 'lemonade', because we knew they were almost as short of money as we were. One Wren once said 'Pimm's Number One', and news of this shocking request spread rapidly from her own Watch, which was Number Two Watch, to all the other Watches, including the one that was on duty at the time.

Sometimes neither we nor our escorts had enough money for cinema seats or dance hall tickets. But 8d provided a couple with two sessions in a fish and chip shop, a penny for chips and penny for tea each time, and a long walk over Oliver's Mount in between.

We had been looking forward to giving some parties of our own, but to our dismay we found, on arrival at the Cecil, that the Mess fund was deeply in debt. We had to spend several months paying off our (Chief Wren) predecessors' debts before there was a surplus for us. We had paid for our Christmas party out of our own pockets, and came to the conclusion, particularly after our Hampshire farming experience, that Mess funds were a dead loss.

Our weekly pay of 16s 4d was supplemented by a clothing allowance of 2s 8d. In the WRNS, after the initial issue of clothing, we were responsible for buying what replacements we needed. A new suit was a fairly big expenditure, and we made earnest calculations of how long the war was likely to last, and whether we could see it through on our existing wardrobe. Although we were in uniform, it was just possible for sudden fashions to engulf us —it was at this time that we all sent home to our mothers to find our old school tunic girdles, which we cut up and used as ties.

Clothing which was not obtainable from Service sources —underclothes and nightclothes—could be bought 'ashore' on 'clothing chits', which were rationed to us, but not very stringently. Sometimes a shop could be persuaded to substitute for the garment named on the chit some other garment of equivalent coupon value, and in this way we did occasionally acquire a pair of civilian shoes, for example (on a 'bedroom slipper' chit), or a blouse instead of vests. But our pay was never intended to cover extravagancies of that kind, so, unlike girls of almost every other generation, we practically never talked about clothes, because we could not have any.

When winter came, the sailors put on their winter over-coats. The significance of this had previously escaped me. A sailor cannot put on his overcoat unaided, as the big Sea-man's collar rides up out of the coat at the back of the neck. Someone, therefore, must put their arms round the sailor from the front and hold his collar down while he gets his coat on. Wrens, it seemed, were specially skilled at holding sailors' collars down. The Seamen did not seem to mind this irritating defect in the construction of their uniforms. Come to that, neither did the Wrens.

As more and more Wrens trained and were drafted to Scarborough, so more and more of the sailors left to go abroad or to join sea-going ships. We bade a tearful farewell to one draft, but they were back inside a week. Their ship had gone without them. Next time they left, it was at twelve hours' notice, and, as some of them were off duty when the message was received, it meant that the canteens all over town had to be scoured for them, and cinema performances interrupted with little notices asking them to return to their base. The Services, as one of them said to me, can be "very exigent". ('The Exigencies of the Service' was a familiar expression with regard to unwelcome orders.)

Then the younger able-bodied civilians at the station were called up. Soon there would be only the Wrens and the most doddery civilians left. The largest, strongest Wrens were selected to train as spare time mechanics, to run the diesel engines which were to power the station if the electricity failed. Secretly I was rather pleased that I was not picked for this job. Perhaps it meant that in other people's eyes I was not quite such a hefty wench as I imagined myself to be.

Hefty or not, I certainly played hockey. The Wrens and the Marines formed a mixed hockey team, and played rough and violent hockey against the other Services. The sailors wanted to play in the team too, but they had no sports clothes. They tried unsuccessfully to borrow from the RAF, and we thought of getting up a charity dance in aid of Shirts and Socks for Sailors, but before we had done anything about it they had been replaced at the station by Wrens. A group of Dutch escapees, training to be pilots, decided to form a hockey team and join the fun, but it was a long time before a match was arranged, as no one could understand what they were saying when, in very broken English, they phoned the Wrennery to offer their challenge.

For no reason that we were aware of, we were sent off on route marches from time to time. On the far side of the park, where the railings had all been removed for war salvage, there was a sharp corner in the road, and bushes in the park. The rear six or nine girls could usually manage to march into the bushes instead of round the corner on the road, which left one free for the rest of the afternoon. Sometimes, instead of our own Chief Petty Officers, young Marines were sent to take us on route marches, and then we trotted obediently behind them all the way. They seemed very young and defenceless, and we did not wish to get them into trouble.

The Marines were bandsmen. They were planning a big concert at the Winter Gardens, and I was asked to do the announcing. I was very excited, and spent days practising how to announce 'Die Fledermaus', but I had overlooked a detail. It was forbidden for WRNS personnel, who were supposed to be elite beyond measure, to appear in uniform on a public platform.

I don't think I had ever known about this rule, and I was bitterly disappointed when, the day before the concert, one of the WRNS officers sent for me and told me that in no circumstances could I announce the names of the works to be played by the Royal Marine Light Classical Orchestra.

Shortly afterwards, one of the cinemas put on a very patriotic programme to celebrate the final conquest of North Africa. The cinema organ played Elgar's *Pomp and Circumstance*, and two representatives of each of the Armed Forces marched onto the stage while we almost shed tears of patriotic ecstasy. Each of the Armed Forces, that is, except the WRNS. We were certainly a very elite service.

In the privacy of our Quarters, however, we organized concert parties and revues for invited guests. I had a piano accordion, with which I enjoyed slaughtering the air waves. It had never been appreciated before. One of the staff at school had said she was 'glad I had a hobby that was different', but she was over eighty, and deaf. At home everyone used to leave the house when I started playing. Once, I said "I think I'm going to sell my piano accordion ..." and they all began to cheer before I had finished the sentence, which was to have ended "and buy a bigger one".

Impromptu concerts used to erupt in the canteens, and then we forgot the rule about not appearing on platforms in uniform and joined in with some of the turns and sketches we had been working out in the privacy of the Wrennery.

During this time, a Lieutenant-Commander visited Scarborough and gave a public talk called 'This Sea Affair of Ours', which he said was a quotation from a letter written by Queen Anne. The Scarborough people were not much interested, and few went to hear him, which was foolish of them, because those of us Wrens who went heard a vivid discourse on what happens when a nation neglects its navy.

He quoted to us Cowper's poem on the loss of the *Royal George, Toll for the Brave,* which described how

A land breeze shook the shrouds
And she was overset.

This gust over the South Downs, said the officer, was a figment of the poet's imagination. He paused and we looked up expectantly. When he was sure that every eye was fixed upon him, he said: "She had not been in dry dock for twenty years, and *her bottom fell out.*"

Never, since that day, have I felt able to overlook the importance of dry docks. He also told us that at the start of World War II he had inspected the guns of his destroyer flotilla. All the gun-barrels had been manufactured before the turn of the century. There was not a twentieth-century barrel among them.

We returned soberly to our work. No wonder there was trouble in the North Atlantic.

Some time during the spring a new naval MO was drafted to Scarborough. He was a tall handsome Canadian, and he had been two years at sea. We had all recovered completely from measles, and were in rude good health, nevertheless the queues outside sick-bay lengthened daily. Many Wrens suddenly thought it was about time they had another typhoid and anti-tetanus injection. I recalled that my vaccination had never 'taken', and I felt in mortal peril of smallpox.

It was well worth it. The new MO was a heart-throb of the first order. When it came to my turn, I handed in my paybook for details of my re-vaccination to be entered. On the front page was a fine drawing of a cowboy, and a poem I had copied out of a magazine because I liked it:

Tear down the tent and the shelter
Stars pale for the breaking of day.
Far over the hills lies Canada
Let us be on our way.

The VAD who took my book studied the first page and was shocked. Naval regulations did not permit defacing the paybook. "Ma'am," she said to the QARNNS sister, "this Wren has cowboys in her paybook." The QARNNS sister took the book and studied it. "Sir," she said to the MO, "this Wren has cowboys in her paybook." The MO took the book.

"Why", he asked, "have you got cowboys in your paybook?"

"Because I like hill-billy songs", I said.

"What's that got to do with it?" said the MO.

"Well, Sir, because cowboys sing hill-billy songs."

"They certainly do not", he said in his lazy Canadian accent. "Cowboys sing cowboy songs. Hill-billies sing hill-billy songs."

"It's the same thing, isn't it?" I said, rather uncertainly now.

The MO said it wasn't. He gave me a lecture on the hill-billies, that they were the poor whites of the Kentucky mountains, and had nothing whatever to do with cowboys.

My new vaccination was cheap at the price. And any-way, it didn't 'take' either.

Typhoid and anti-tetanus injections, however, could be guaranteed to produce an effect. If nothing else happened, at least one's arm became too stiff and sore to be lifted. This did not trouble us particularly, as it was not too difficult to put on our WRNS shirts and jackets without lifting our arms, but it was a different matter for the Seamen, whose tight-fitting jumpers had no zips or other openings, and had to be wriggled into like a second skin. We were very sorry for them. The Army girls, we heard, had forty-eight hours compulsory CB (Confined to Barracks) after injections. We went straight back on watch, day or night. We did not envy them. We thought them molly-coddled.

A slight murmuring began among us that spring, as we thought it was about time somebody was promoted. There were about a hundred and fifty of us Wren telegraphists at work, and not a Leading Wren among us. The few girls who had dropped out of W/T through ear trouble, inability to sleep during the day, or just plain surfeit of Morse, had raced ahead of us in the other categories to which they had trans-ferred, and one, by changing into another branch, had even got herself commissioned.

An exam was arranged for us.

Many of us had been consolidating our knowledge of wireless telegraphy by attending evening classes on electricity at the local technical college. In company with a group of schoolboy apprentices, we had chased ball-bearings round the tables with magnets, and been initiated into magnetic fields, north and south magnetic poles, neutrons, protons and electrons. This was work beyond the call of duty, however, so far as promotion was concerned, as the

Leading Rate exam was a simple speed and accuracy test at twenty-five words per minute.

But spring passed into summer, and still nobody achieved the coveted promotion. Then came news that the exam we had done was not valid: we had done it at twenty-five wpm, but should only have been tested at twenty-three. The logic of requiring a fresh exam on these grounds escaped us, but in June we took a second exam, this time with a few written papers thrown in.

Before there had been any outcome to this development, a flurry of excitement convulsed the many Wrenneries of northern Scarborough. A draft of six Wrens was required for overseas service.

Many of us had volunteered for service abroad over the course of the last year. Those under twenty-one had to have their parents' consent. Of my close friends, Rachel and Joy had obtained parental permission, but Gay, who was nineteen, was not successful. It was only a few months since her brother had been lost at sea, so she did not nag her parents to let her go. My path was not unobstructed, as my mother said that it was little more than a year since I had left boarding school, and I knew far too little of the ways of the world for her to sanction my being sent abroad.

"Well I don't know", my father had said. "If she were a boy we could not keep her at home, and I don't see why, just because she's a girl, we should stand in her way. She only needs one parent's consent, and I'll give mine."

So my mother acquiesced, and I got the necessary permission.

Interviewing began among a short-list of thirty-two Wrens, all of whom had stood well in the recent L/W exams. Interviews and medicals pared the list down to the necessary six, all of us from the first group to pass out from the Signal School the previous year. Besides myself (by now the only under-twenty-one), Rachel, Beryl, Sheila, Doris and Havoc were selected.

"Can you say where you're going?" asked my mother when I went home on embarkation leave. "We don't know where we're going," I replied, "and as long as it's not Gibraltar we don't mind." We had to report to a drafting depot in Golden Square, London. There were, we found, six more telegraphists from the R.N. Shore Wireless station outside Winchester, who were part of our draft, and, having trained later than us, were able to update us on the development of the Mess Fund Farm. Altogether there were five separate drafts at the depot, about a hundred and thirty Wrens in all, presumably headed for five separate destinations. What those destinations were, nobody knew.

We sat on our beds mulling over our possible future home. We mentioned Mombasa, Colombo and Alexandria. Somebody remembered that there were Wren telegraphists in Gibraltar. One of the first overseas drafts of the war had been of telegraphists bound for Gibraltar. All had been lost at sea, and twelve replacements had been sent out. Those replacements had now served two years abroad, and we wondered whether we were to relieve them. Fervently we hoped not. The Rock had a bad name among Wrens.

Then came another mystery. We were issued with thirty-five clothing coupons, and told to go out and spend them. There was much further speculation: did this mean we were going to a neutral country, where we would have to wear civilian clothing? Even, into occupied territory? In which case, if discovered, we should be shot, as Service people masquerading in civilian clothes in enemy territory were regarded as spies. Were we headed for Iceland? Or the Tropics? Furs or bathing suits?

We reported back to the officer in charge of the drafting depot, and explained our dilemma. She thought for a moment.

"On the whole," she said, "I should recommend you to prepare for warm weather, and to shop with your off-duty hours in mind."

This sounded ominous. It sounded as if our destination was indeed Gibraltar, where, we had heard, there was absolutely nothing for a rating to do, and nowhere to go, as all reputable restaurants and hotels were reserved for officers only. Authority had, as a special concession, given WRNS ratings permission to wear civilian clothes to permit them to enter such establishments if invited to do so by an officer.

Not knowing how soon we should be despatched to join a ship, we shopped hectically in the West End with our thirty-five coupons. We were all looking for an evening dress, but there were hardly any to be had, and nothing under £10, which was more than any of us could afford. Thirty-five coupons was all very fine, but we had hardly any money with which to spend them. It cost me three weeks' pay to buy a suitcase from the railway lost property shop. In the end, I bought a cheap, light, pretty summer dressing gown for £3. I sewed up the front, cut off the top, and ended up with a gay and dainty tropical evening dress. A cotton frock, some tropical-weight underclothes, white shirts and shorts in case we played tennis, a bathing dress, and our exotic wardrobe was complete.

Then came kitting-up with our uniform tropical kit. To our horror, we were reissued with the old pudding bowl hats, embellished now with a white cotton pull-on top. These were to shelter us from sun more adequately than our sailor caps. White dresses, white skirts and blouses, white lisle stockings and socks, and flat white lace-up canvas shoes followed, plus a kit-bag in which to put it all, a topee, and a tin mug. We pushed all the kit into the kit-bag, topped it off with the topee, tied the tin mug on the top, and were about to set off back across London to the drafting depot when we remembered something.

Only Wrens on overseas draft had tin mugs. It would be obvious to the whole world the moment we dragged our kit-bags out into the street that we were going abroad, and that would mean the U-boats would be forewarned that a

convoy was about to sail. We undid our kit-bags and concealed the tin mugs inside. We overlooked the fact that only
Wrens on overseas draft had kit-bags, either.

Various admonitory lectures were arranged for us before
we left. Those of us who had been home on embarkation
leave had already had them from our parents. A naval
chaplain spoke to us, and so did a WRNS Superintendent,
who told us that overseas tended to be very romantic, what
with palm trees and all that, and we must be on our guard
against our feelings.

"Please don't get into trouble", she said. "We do not
want to be bothered with shipping you home before your
tour of duty is complete." She also told us that sunstroke
was caused by loss of salt when one sweated, and that if we
put salt in our drinks we should find them much more
refreshing, an interesting point which my father had not
included in his parting lecture.

So we prepared to go abroad with two ideas very clear in
our minds. We must not get into trouble; and we must put a
pinch of salt in our lemonade.

But day succeeded day and we did not go. We went to
church parade at St. George's Hanover Square. We had very
little money left—some were cleaned right out by the
shopping spree for civilian clothes. The six of us from
Scarborough decided to pool our remaining resources and
have a final celebration. We bought a box of chocolates and
six seats for *The Moon is Down*. After that there was still just
enough left to buy us chips and salad at a café in Leicester
Square. If we did not go the following day, we should just
have to sit in till the next pay day.

But the following evening lorries came to the drafting
depot, and we were driven to a busy London railway
terminus, unidentified of course, as was the usual wartime
practice (I've little doubt it was Euston). Wrens and sailors
were milling everywhere, on platforms stacked with crates
of summer fruit, ready to board the 'ghost train' which left
each night for an unknown destination. It was July, and

double-summer-time, so although it was quite late the sun was still prominent, and we could tell that we were travelling north, but that was all we knew. Seated in our small carriage, four-a-side, we fell asleep. The overseas adventure had begun.

Chapter VI

In Convoy

Next morning we were standing in warm sunlight on the bank of the Clyde. Out on the dancing water, great ships shone in the sun. We boarded a tender, and were put aboard a Dutch ship, the *Indrapoera*, with a Dutch East Indies crew. Our quarters were to be in the ship's hospital, and we were to eat in the officers' Mess.

It was unbelievably luxurious. Dark-skinned waiters brought us our food, the bread on the table was of a whiteness we had not seen since the grey national loaf came in, and there were table napkins.

It was all a bit of a strain. Back at the Wrennery there had never been enough cutlery to go round, and it was second nature to us to use the sugar spoon for stirring our coffee and then put it back in the sugar bowl; to use the same knife for cutting meat and spreading jam. We tried to remember our manners, but at the end of the first meal we automatically piled all our plates, cups and saucers on top of one another ready to sweep them all to the galley for washing-up. This was not considered appropriate in the officers' Mess.

Before we had adjusted to living like ladies, the tender returned and we all disembarked again, accompanied by some hundreds of troops who were also on board, though less palatially accommodated. It seems that there was some doubt as to the loyalty of the East Indies crew. A sister ship had recently put to sea and been sabotaged, so our ship was not, after all, to sail with the convoy in case she suffered the same fate. We were transferred to a 24,000-ton British liner, *RMS Orion* of the Orient line. (*Indrapoera* must have overcome her problems. Years later I happened to find out from contemporaries who served in Colombo that the prisoners-of-war released from Japanese camps whom they met in 1945 were returning home aboard the *Indrapoera*.)

RMS Orion was already full when we joined her. This time we were to travel as NCOs. Seven of us were squeezed into a cabin intended for two peace-time passengers, but two extra double bunks had been crammed in, so only one had to sleep on the floor, and this we took it in turns to do.* We were young and slept well on a mattress on the floor, but it was an unpopular berth because of the livestock, mostly cockroaches, with which the floor became populated after dark. We had an insect-repellent powder, a less effective forerunner of DDT (not yet on the market), and with this we built little walls round the mattress.

Before our final selection for overseas service, Rachel had very nearly gone back on the whole idea because of creepy crawlies. We knew that they abounded overseas—not just mosquitoes and ants and cockroaches, which were bad enough, but scorpions and really large spiders. I scoffed at Rachel for this weakness, but when we came face to face with them I was as helpless as she was, and we simply clung to one another shouting for help until someone more sensible, Havoc for instance, or Beryl, came and rescued us from peril.

The *Orion* must have carried thousands of cockroaches. They turned up everywhere. They bobbed against our lips when we drank coffee, in which they were invisible as tea and coffee were served black (there was no available milk). They turned up boiled in stewed apple and stewed rhubarb,

---

* *Wikipedia* states that her pre-war capacity was 486 First Class passengers, 653 Tourist Class. When used for cruising, it was 600. In 1943 she was carrying 7,000 troops at a time.

in which they looked very like dates, which were often used for sweetening at the time because of the shortage of sugar.

On the whole, though, we had little to complain of. It was different for the troops, already overcrowded before the drafts from the Dutch ship were added. Packed in a sweating mass below decks, they were lucky if they got any food at all as, in the confusion of their cramped Messes, a moment's inattention meant that someone else was eating up their dinner. It was a case of devil take the hindmost.

Whatever conditions may have been like inside those shining hulls, externally we presented a brave appearance. When we sailed, fourteen other great ships sailed with us, three abreast, five deep, out into the Atlantic. A huge deployment of troops—going where? When we had been about four days at sea, we learnt that our own destination was indeed to be Gibraltar. We were the reliefs for the dozen Chief Wrens who, in 1941, had replaced the original draft, all of whom had been lost at sea in August of 1941. *RMS Orion*, however, was not going there direct. We were loaded with troops for the First Army in North Africa, and we were bound for Algiers. Round us were dotted our escort: an aircraft carrier, a cruiser, destroyers, frigates and sloops.

We did not know it at the time, but post-war intelligence publications revealed that the summer of 1943 marked the turning of the tide in the Battle of the Atlantic. With thirty per cent of the U-boats at sea being destroyed, Admiral Doenitz withdrew the main concentration from the North Atlantic to the Azores and the Bay of Biscay. To this area we were now sailing. Eighty-six U-boats crossed the Bay during July, and twenty of them were destroyed. Between July 19th, when we sailed, and August 2nd when we reached Oran, ten U-boats were sunk in the vicinity of the Bay. We knew nothing of it. Occasionally we heard depth charges being dropped, but our escort protected us completely.

We wondered who they were, those grey watchdogs on the horizon. Later on, after we docked at Gib, we were accosted in the street by a young sailor who had noticed our pale faces among the tanned inhabitants of the Rock.

"You've only just arrived!" he said triumphantly. "Did you come off that convoy?"

"Yes", we said. He was about nineteen, fair-haired and slim, and he had green eyes.

"We were your escort", he said proudly.

"Who are you?" I asked. His cap showed only the regulation *HMS*.

"*Egret*", he said.

We knew the name. *Egret* and her sister ship *Pelican*, also one of our escort, had taken part a few weeks' previously in a hard-fought Atlantic battle that brought a big convoy from the United States under heavy attack. The news had just been released on the BBC.

"We'll be back in Gib", said the sailor. "I'll see you, Jenny."

But I never saw him again. *Egret* sailed for the Bay, and two weeks later, off Portugal, she went to the bottom, the first British warship to be destroyed by a radio-controlled flying bomb.

Throughout the journey we zig-zagged. *Orion* was commodore's ship, and pooped the commands to alter course. She would give one sharp blast, and a few seconds later the assembled great liners would alter course to starboard, and the creamy wakes would curve away behind us. So we would continue until our ship gave the double blast that brought the alteration to port.

To avoid attracting the attention of U-boats, we were forbidden to throw overboard any sort of rubbish or refuse. Matches and empty cigarette cartons had to be hoarded. Private wireless sets were forbidden, as even a receiver generates a slight but perceptible electrical impulse which could be used as a guide by the enemy.

We spent about two hours a day practising 'action stations' and 'emergency stations'. On 'action stations' we went to our cabins, put on the lifebelts which we carried with us wherever we went, and stayed there out of the way. On the 'emergency stations' warning, we tore up to our various lifeboat stations and were instructed in the usual arts of tying our lifebelts in such a way that they would not bounce up and break our necks if we had to jump into the water. The belts had little red lights on them, so that we should show up at night in the water.

At night, no matter how warm it grew as we zig-zagged south, we were ordered to wear our sweaters and bell-bottomed trousers, ready to abandon ship, and to keep our greatcoats by us. Most of us wore money-belts next to our skin at night, but the rest of our valuables were crammed into our greatcoat pockets, which fortunately were very capacious. My provisions for shipwreck, stowed in my greatcoat pockets, consisted of a bar of sea soap (which was supposed to lather in salt water), a clean hanky, a pair of socks, two pairs of gloves, a torch, naval issue anti-mosquito cream, anti-sunburn cream, shipwreck rations, two bars of chocolate, half a pound a toffees, an imitation pearl necklace, as much toilet paper as I could stuff into the remaining space in the pockets, and my PAYBOOK. The most essential thing, as we knew, was the paybook. It must not be left floating about at the scene of a sinking, otherwise the enemy would fish it out and use it to equip a spy. If we went to the bottom, we must see to it that the paybook went with us.

Although bell-bottoms were compulsory at night, they were forbidden during the day. This order caused discontent. A troopship, however luxurious her peace-time standards, is not a luxury liner. We could lie on our bunks in our airless cabin, or we could walk about the deck, crowded so thick with troops that one almost had to queue for a chance to see over the rail. What we could not do was sit down; this was not the sort of voyage that sported deck chairs. There were chairs in the officers' lounge, and we were permitted to go and sit on them if invited to do so, but there were plenty of officers already on them, and it was embarrassing to stand about at the door of the lounge waiting to be invited in.

Besides, within a day or two we had struck up friendships with some of the troops, whose company we did not wish to forego.

Of course one could always sit down on the deck, but that was why we wanted to wear trousers. Sitting on the deck in a narrow white drill skirt soon becomes either comfortable but indecent or respectable but tortuous. Some of us chose comfort, and some chose respectability. All railed at an order which condemned us to make the choice. It takes a man's clothing to lead a man's life.

There was a large contingent of paratroopers on board. They were exuberant and irrepressible. They staged impromptu concert parties, boxing matches and sessions of a game which I though must be named after a man called Tom Bowler. Largest and most exuberant was a Jewish cockney named Jerry, who decided what we were all going to do next. His aide was a small soldier composed mostly of teeth, who never spoke until Jerry had decided on the programme for the morning, after which Fred thought out all the detailed plans and ideas. The paratroop intellectual, Stan, kept a copy of the works of Karel Capek in his hand, and read it when the maelstrom on deck abated sufficiently (I've still got it. He gave it to me just before they disembarked in Algiers). He had a namesake, Little Stan, who was so small, so young, and so boyish that none of us could bear the thought that he was off to fight, and he was unmercifully mothered by all the Wrens in turn.

The paratroopers were followed round all day by a sub-mariner called Curly, who had a white turtle-necked sub-mariners' sweater that reached to his knees. He wore it rolled up to his hips, storing at each turn his handkerchief, money, cigarettes, matches, and anything else he wanted. If you asked Curly for a light he very willingly began to unroll his sweater, and a cascade of his possessions would begin to shower out at various levels on to the deck.

Alone among this boisterous bunch, a nineteen-year-old soldier from Yorkshire, in the maroon beret of the Parachute

Regiment, stood at the rail and gazed at the merchant ship keeping her station on our port beam. She was laden with some kind of equipment, and from her after-deck a forest of spars rose up. There were crossbeams on the spars, so that she looked like an overcrowded cemetery, and as evening came and the eastern sky grew dark, the crosses shone out in the straight rays of the setting sun.

"One of them is for me", said the boy from Yorkshire quietly. "I never wanted to come."

In the evenings we settled on the crowded decks and sang. Darkness came, and the crisp outlines of the distant destroyer escort merged with the horizon. Then the merchant ships of the convoy gradually disappeared into the night, and only the flowing phosphorous showed where fifteen great liners ploughed south through the Atlantic. The Yugoslav who had escaped from half the prisons of Europe in his effort to reach England picked up his guitar and sang the folk songs of his native land, and the mysterious soldier with him, who spoke broken English and would never say where his home had been, sang in broken Spanish. The paratroopers stopped their fooling and applauded the Seamen who sang with such sincerity 'Bless This House', and 'This is Worth Fighting For'. They even dropped their casual feud with the American troops and let them sing their carefully harmonized barber-shop songs without feeling obliged to break it up with a peculiarly raucous version of 'Knees Up Mother Brown', which was their day-time response to any American attempt to sing.

The Americans were prisoner-of-war guards. They were almost permanently at sea escorting batches of prisoners-of-war to their camps, mostly in North America. They were constantly on the move, and their mail had not caught up with them for six months. One of them, a young sergeant named Bill, had been due to become a father during those six months, but whether his child was a boy or girl he did not know.

Sergeant Bill was appalled that we were being sent over-seas. We were, in his estimation, far too young and innocent.

"You'll meet nothing but unscrupulous men who think you're there for one purpose and one purpose only", he said. "Don't drink. For God's sake don't drink. If you'd seen what I've seen in the VD hospitals in North Africa … Look, just *don't drink*. That's all."

We thanked him for his warnings, and said we would remember what he said.

"You're just a lot of babes in the wood", said Sergeant Bill. He was all of twenty-five himself.

We did a little work on board. Every day, to keep us in practice, the telegraphists reported to the wireless cabin and the Marconi officer gave us Morse exercises. Daily the cruiser who formed part of our escort (*Charybdis* we learned later) flashed aldis signals to our ship, and these we read, but with difficulty. Morse through the eyes evoked none of the automatic response of Morse through the ears.

On our seventh day out the convoy divided. *Orion* and seven other liners, with the cruiser, two sloops and three frigates, turned east towards the Med, leaving the rest of the convoy to sail on south to the Cape. On our ninth day at sea the coast of North Africa appeared, and soon we were anchored in Algiers. The buildings shone square and white in the dazzling sun of midsummer, and behind them the hills sweltered, grey-brown and olive. Army trucks littered the wide areas of the quay, Army stores were piled on every side. And for two days a thick stream of khaki disgorged from the steaming holds of *RMS Orion*.

On the afternoon of the second day we were allowed ashore. Daintily, in our new white tropical uniform, we picked our way across the quay and walked into the town.

It was very disappointing. There were no dashing sheiks to be seen, no Arab horses, and no beautiful women flashing almond eyes above jewelled yashmaks. Nothing but filthy ragged people in cast-off remnants of western clothing, who leered at us and asked for money, women with grubby snot-stained pocket-handkerchiefs pinned across their faces, shops devoid of anything but sticky sweetmeats laden with flies, and over all the acrid pervasive smell of stale urine. Everywhere an indefinable aura of hostility surrounded us.

Overseas did not seem so very romantic after all. We looked for a restaurant, but could find nowhere to eat, so returned to the stewed cockroaches on board.

Next day the stream of khaki reversed, and flowed from the quay into the ship. It was a ragged but cheerful stream. It was composed of Italian prisoners-of-war, very happy to have come to the end of their fighting days. From time to time the stream was interrupted, and a small covey of smart, morose officers of the Afrika Korps marched on board and headed up to A deck, where we affected not to see them. (Being on A Deck was a new departure for us; it had been reserved for 'Officers Only' prior to our arrival in Algiers.) Not by so much as a glance would we fraternize with the enemy.

Some NCOs of the First Army came aboard, going back to the UK for various reasons (usually to be commissioned), and we commiserated with them for the hostility of the French which we had sensed in Algiers. They corrected us. They were serving with the French up at the Front, and found them the best of allies. It was not French hostility that we had sensed in Algiers, but Arab.

For two days the prisoners-of-war streamed into *Orion*. On our last evening in Algiers we went ashore with a party of Canadian Air Force pilots. They took us to the Allied Officers Club, but after 10 minutes a WRNS officer notified the management that we were not officers, and we were ignominiously ejected into the streets again. We had trespassed too far in thinking that permission to sit on officers' chairs, if invited to do so, extended ashore. Finally we found a not-too-disreputable bar, and settled down for the evening.

Our party was joined by several American officers. Somebody mentioned the word 'candy'. It was a word that held a certain mystery for me as, years before, a Canadian visitor to our house had given me a bar of a brownish, sweet substance, telling me it was 'candy'. I thought 'candy' was a specific term, like 'chocolate', or 'butterscotch', not realizing that North Americans use the term much as we use 'sweet'. I had never seen 'candy' again, and had always wondered what it was. Now was my chance to find out.

"What is candy?" I asked the American.

"You don't know what candy is!" he expostulated.

"No. I had some once, but ...'

A somewhat beady look formed in the American's eyes.

"I've got loads of candy in my apartment", he said.

"Have you? Well, I was wondering what it was, because ..."

"If you care to come along to my apartment, I'll give you any amount."

"Oh," I said, "that's very nice of you. Are you sure you can spare it?"

"Sure," said the American, "come on, let's go."

We had come ashore under the care of a PO Wren, and we had to go back on board when she went back. She was hemmed against the wall on the far side of the bar, and the space between us was packed solid with sweating humanity. To squeeze through and ask her if I had got time to go off with an American officer to his apartment would be a monumental effort, and then she might say no.

"I'm supposed to stay with the Petty Officer", I said. "I don't think I'd better come. Couldn't you nip back and fetch some?"

The officer did not think he could. It was too far. That settled things in my mind, as if it was too far for him, it was too far for me, too. The opportunity to find out what 'candy' was would just have to be lost. (It was another ten years before I found out what it was I had been given, when a French-Canadian girl gave me a maple leaf made of crystallized maple sugar.)

The evening passed, and the Petty Officer collected us together to return to the ship. The American officer escorted me to the quay, shook my hand, and said goodbye.

"It's been nice knowing you, kid," he said, "there aren't many like you."

I wondered what he could possibly mean.

Someone in the bar had given us each a bunch of roses. Clasping them in our sticky hands, we toiled up the gang-plank. At the top, trouble awaited us. A very young Duty Officer was very angry.

"You're all adrift", he said.

"Oh no", we protested. We had all been as good as gold, we had stayed with the Petty Officer, and … He cut us short.

"These Wrens are all defaulters", he said to the Duty Petty Officer. "Fall them in." And he went away.

"Get fell in", said the Duty PO wearily. He sounded as if he had had a tiring day.

We got fell in.

"Wrens … 'Shun", said the Duty PO.

We came to attention. At least, our feet did, but our hands could not, as we were all holding roses.

"You can't hang on to them roses. Put them down", said the Duty PO.

We protested. If we put our roses down, no one would know which roses were which. We were all very attached to our own particular roses, and we did not want them muddled up. In the middle of these protestations, the Duty Officer returned.

"Are those Wrens ready yet?" he asked.

The Duty PO sighed.

"I can't make them put their roses down, Sir", he said in an aggrieved tone.

The Duty Officer was possibly regretting the whole episode.

"Oh never mind," he said, "I'll talk to them as they are."

The Duty PO turned to address us again.

"Wren platoon," he shouted, "OFF … CAPS."

This was an astonishing order. It had never been addressed to us before. Seamen whipped their caps off at various times, such as when being reprimanded, but it was not part of the drill for Wrens to do so. However, we saw that it would have its advantages on this occasion, as we could all recognize our own hats (tropical uniform had put us back into pudding-bowls with brims), and by putting our own roses in our own hats we should be able to please the Petty Officer and also assure continued ownership of our own roses. Carefully, so as not to spoil our hair-dos, we removed our hats, broke ranks, lined the hats up along the bulkhead with a bunch of roses in each, and 'got fell in' again.

It seemed that we had all returned to the ship at the hour prescribed for Petty Officers, whereas we should have returned 30 minutes prior to the Petty Officer in whose charge we'd gone ashore. We pleaded ignorance and were told not to do it again.

"ON ... CAPS", shouted the Duty PO.

We broke ranks again and collected our hats. We began to put them on again, but it took some time, as there were curls to be arranged, and the task, in the absence of looking glasses, of checking one another to see that the *HMS* was properly sited in the middle of the front. At last all was in order, and we were dismissed to our cabins.

We were not the only ones who had spent the evening ashore. A procession of our fellow passengers began to arrive in our companionway, all somewhat the worse for wear, and all intent on calling on a favourite Wren. The Petty Officer who had shepherded us ashore coped nobly for a while, but finally there was only one thing for it. A sentry was posted and, for the first but not the last time, we slept under armed guard. As Sergeant Bill had said, liquor was a terrible thing.

Next day we left Algiers, but not, as we had thought, for Gibraltar. The following dawn found us steaming by a long, high, sandy escarpment, on top of which, black against the bright eastern sky, were palm trees and Arab tents, and as the sun climbed higher and the daylight crept down the sandy slopes, we saw that perched on ledges of the cliffs were more tents and palm trees and tiny black figures. We were entering Oran.

We remained at anchor off Oran all day. Like Adlestrop station, no one left and no one came. The African sun blazed down. Some American sailors in a battered US Navy ship lolled at the rail and spat the remains of their chewing gum into the water. Little fish swam up and down beside us. A thin film of oil floated by. We were bored.

The Italian POWs made themselves very much at home, burst into song, and began to wait at table. The Afrika Korps officers continued to march sullenly to and fro on A Deck. Between lunch and tea, for the sake of something to do, we opened our tins of shipwreck rations.

Inside was a cake of a thick chocolaty substance, marked off in squares. Each square was about the size of half a matchbox, and was supposed to last a day. It looked quite appetizing, and we ate it. After that we had to spend the rest of the day marching up and down behind the Germans, as the shipwreck rations swelled up abominably in our insides.

"The U-boats are lying in wait for us off Gib," we heard, "so we're going to sit in Oran till they go." They must have gone next day, for we sailed again, retracing our course west through the Mediterranean.*

On August 4th, nineteen days after we left the quay-side on the Clyde, we reached our destination. It was early morning, and the ship lay anchored in Gibraltar harbour, on

---

* *Wikipedia* provides an account of an Italian miniature submarine depot ship, the *Olterra*, moored in Algeciras opposite Gibraltar, from which during the night of August 3rd/4th attacks were launched on shipping in Gibraltar Bay that resulted in the destruction of three supply ships: an American vessel of 7,700 tons, a Norwegian of 9,900 tons, and a British of 6,000 tons, a total of over 23,000 tons. Was foreknowledge of this intended activity involved in the decision to keep us dallying in Oran? If so, how was the intelligence derived? Perhaps our Y-Branch had been involved?

the western side of the Rock. We were in a deep cold shadow, for the sun had not yet climbed above the high ridge that is Gibraltar. Above us, on top of us almost, crushing us back into the oily waters of the harbour, the Rock rose black and faintly menacing.

We had arrived; but there was something slightly ominous about those first moments in our new home.

Chapter VII

The Rock

Within a few hours of arriving in Gibraltar we were trying to reconcile ourselves to the thought of dying young. Our work awaited us in an eyrie on the top of the Rock, where the wireless station had been established. Between this and our Quarters in town on the west stretched a single-track road composed of hairpin bends, half-forgotten landslides, and steep ascents so placed that the necessary acceleration had to be made round a blind corner.

Our first ride up was unforgettable. As we soared towards the sky, range on range of hills detached themselves from the Spanish horizon and showed brown and orange in the parched foreground, blue and purple in the distance. We made the journey in silence. It was not so much wonder at the beauties of nature, here spread before us, that kept us quiet—indeed Rachel and Doris had their eyes shut. We were paralysed with fear. Precipices fell away beside us, our speed never slackened, and we did not expect to complete the journey alive. (In the end the transport did go over the edge of the Rock, but no one was hurt as only the driver was in it at the time, and he jumped clear.)

Whatever doubts we may have had on disembarkation, our first night duty reconciled us to our new location. The watch changed at midnight, and before taking over we stood for a few moments looking over the Bay. Down in the town below us the lights blazed. There was no black-out of the lower Rock; only the upper slopes were silent and lightless, the position of the gun sites being a security secret. Far to the

left across the Mediterranean a pin prick of light shone from
Ceuta in Spanish Morocco; ahead the lights of Algeciras
danced and twinkled from the Andalusian shore of the Bay;
to the right, in Spain beyond the isthmus, the lights of La
Linea glowed, steady and unblinking. There was always that
difference between Algeciras and La Linea, the one
twinkling, the other glowing. 'Algeciras is on AC and La
Linea is on DC', we used to say facetiously, rather pleased
with ourselves for thinking of an Electrical Joke, but I think
the true explanation must have been that we looked at
Algeciras across the roof tops of Gibraltar, and probably the
air above the town was still hot and shimmering.

As we stood in the darkness on the top of the Rock,
searchlights swept across the Bay, trapping in a moment's
clear detail the great ships that lay at anchor. A late ship stole
in from the Straits, like a star sliding over the black water, a
second star rippling below her where the mast-head light
was reflected. We were much moved to think that we were
helping to garrison such a place, and dashed off one or two
rather patriotic poems.

A certain patriotic fervour was a help, for apart from the
view, our wireless station had very little to commend it.
Several caves had been hollowed out on the eastern side of
the Rock, lined with nissen, and finished by windows and
doors at the front. Two of the caves were occupied by the
Navy, one for the wireless watch-room and one for some
electrical equipment, there being sufficient space to add
three pallets on the floor on which we slept when on stand-
by duty. The narrow path fronting the caves was edged by a
parapet below which the eastern side of the Rock consisted
almost entirely of a virtually inaccessible escarpment. Precipices plunged to the sea from heights of up to a thousand
feet, and where the land sloped sufficiently to allow of any
human control, acres of concrete rain catchments had been
constructed (rain being virtually Gibraltar's only source of
fresh water).

The elevation exposed us to the hazard of the Levanter. When the wind came from the hot east across the sea, and was then forced sharply up the eastern escarpment of the Rock, it formed a heavy fog-like cloud of condensation at the top, which cast the whole town into murkiness, and up at the top drenched both us and our bedding. Seen from a distance, away from the Rock, the clouds made by the Levanter seemed like a stationary plume striking hori-zontally out from the top of the Rock across the Bay, but we who were in it knew that it was formed by winds of almost gale-force strength in which we battled, bent, beside the parapet, fighting to get the door shut in the teeth of the gale, condensation forming and dissolving to form the seeming stationary plume.

The watch-keeping pattern to which we had been accustomed at Scarborough could no longer be worked, because, normal car headlights being forbidden on the upper Rock, transport was impossible after dark, and we went on to a system whereby two watches covered each twenty-four-hour period, from 1330 to 1330 the following day, sleeping and eating at the station during their twenty-four hours on duty. The transport (not a lorry, but a van with seats) took three girls up for the 1330 change over, they were relieved at 1800 by their associated watch, bringing with them from the Wrennery a cooked supper. The watch coming off duty ate the supper in the station's office, then turned in for what sleep they could get until midnight, when the two watches changed over. The pallets were immediately re-occupied by the relieved watch, who would return to duty the next morning for the 0800 to 1330 watch. The night watch then went in daylight back down to the Wrennery to sleep. At mid-day the other two watches repeated the sequence, covering the next twenty-four hours. The total hours worked were exactly the same as in Britain, but the arrangement meant we no longer had any days clear of duties, so no more 'stand-offs'.

Off duty, too, our home was a Nissen hut. The 'Old Naval Hospital', a large old house on the southern edge of Gibraltar Town, had become a Wrennery, but the main accommodation was in the six Nissen huts which had been sited in the old central patio. Each hut held 12 beds, real beds not bunks, each with its mosquito net. The corrugated iron roofs broiled in the sun, and the temperature inside the huts rose accordingly. The sun of Gibraltar was surprisingly hot. The pavements burned the soles of our feet through our shoes until we learnt to wear socks, and the sand on the beaches was too hot for walking barefoot. In wet weather, however, the rain poured through the joins in the hut roof, and we paddled from bed to bed reminding ourselves that in Gib fresh water was a luxury. We were a little uncertain about our hut. With hesitant affection, we carved and painted a beautiful sign saying 'Mugshaven', which we put up over the door, but our officers were not amused, and we were ordered to take it down.

The Fortress of Gibraltar, of whose garrison we now formed a part, consisted of rather less than two square miles of unstable shale over limestone, with the well-recognized perpendicular high cliff jutting not, as one had mistakenly supposed, from the sea, but from the northern isthmus joining Gib to Spain, where land reclaimed from the sea had permitted the construction of runways to form an aerodrome. Gibraltar harbour lay in a deep bay, of which the far side, with the town of Algeciras, stretched further south towards North Africa than did Gibraltar itself, so one could not see the Atlantic; only east, down the Mediterranean, did one gaze at sea to the horizon. South, eleven miles away, was the Barbary Coast of Africa, with Apes Hill, which, with the Rock, formed the ancient Pillars of Hercules. The blue hills of Africa seemed to belong to another world, not only because there was always mist at their base, so that they seemed to be floating, detached, but because we could never travel there — nor to anywhere outside Gib itself. Our two square miles formed our total world. It was, to some extent, a prison.

The instability of the shale meant that, contrary to expectation, the Rock was anything but solid. Stone pine and wild olive could not bind the scree, and scrambling about could easily produce a nasty avalanche of slatey chips. It was supposedly for this reason that the noise of motor horns was forbidden. Drivers announced their approach by hammering on the outside of the car door with their fists. Consequently, none of the vehicles in Gib had any paint left in the centre of the driver's door.

There was a tiny fishing community called Catalan Bay between the precipices and the catchments on the eastern side of the Rock. Attempts to build a road to it had been defeated by landslides, and quantities of lorries and equipment were reputedly buried under mounds of shale. Finally the Royal Engineers bored a tunnel.

The newest tunnel-road led from the town to a sandy bay on the Mediterranean side enabling us to nip quickly over for a clean swim, away from the oily deposits from the harbour that tended to foul the rocks on our west side. The tunnel was single width, about eight feet wide and eight feet high, and military police at the entrance controlled the traffic. Once inside, riding in the back of open lorries, our safety was in our own hands, as we attempted to spot the wires trailing below the ceiling in time to avert decapitation. Occasional faint light bulbs at widely spaced intervals were the only light we had, and, as the lorries lurched over the uneven ground where puddles collected from the dripping walls, warning shouts from the lorry ahead would ring back to us, and we would crouch down on the floor while the wires grazed our backs.

In fact, tunnelling became the main occupation of the troops on the Rock. The first tunnels had been made by the Sappers during the Great Siege of 1779–1783, but the real impetus to retreat *inside* the Rock, as distinct from burrowing *through* for the purpose of communicating with the other side, came with the Fall of France in 1940. Gibraltar's tiny two square miles commanding the entrance to the Mediterranean soon became the only allied-held territory in the whole continent of Europe, and they were separated from the Nazi armies by a hostile, Axis-orientated Spain which had coveted the Rock ever since it fell to Britain in 1704. Across the Bay, on the Tarifa Hills in Spain, big siege guns were mounted, pointing at Gib. Over twenty-five miles of tunnels were bored into the Rock. Chambers were hollowed out to house Service headquarters and arsenals. A 200-foot long hospital was constructed, a laundry and a convalescent home, and, because the limestone exuded water all the time, every wall had to be faced. The 1.75 million tons of rubble removed from inside the Rock went to form the runways at the aerodrome.

The troops who carried out the tunnelling were the Royal Engineers, and the Royal Canadian Engineers. There were hard-rock miners from every Province in Canada, coal miners from all over Britain, and the officers included among them some of the finest mining engineers in the country. In the Mediterranean heat they lived in a perpetual film of grey dust, glued to their bodies with sweat and washed off with the sticky salt sea water that was all we had for washing or bathing, fresh water being too precious to use for mere ablutions.

One day during this intense tunnelling activity, a mine truck went off the rails, and, to everyone's amazement, fell through the floor, revealing one of the vast natural cavities with which the Rock is honeycombed. Rachel and I went on a potholing expedition down a rope thrown through the hole where the truck had fallen. Guided by two of the Royal Engineers, and needing hands and feet free to scramble, we tied torches round our necks, and explored the weird world of the troglodyte. Squeezing through narrow cracks, crouching against the rock across wet slopes where the water fell away into gulleys that our torches could not fathom, we made our way past pillared galleries to a great chamber where fluted columns streaked in red and green rose from the edges of a subterranean lake. We probed its black surface with our torches, but its farther shore was beyond their range of light. Above the lake, chandeliers formed by the stalactites hung from the ceiling. And at our feet was (we learned later) something like 70,000 gallons of precious fresh water.

Water was our great problem. For fresh water we depended on rain, and in addition to the big City catchments, every building made arrangements to use its roof as a catchment area, and every little raindrop that fell was zealously collected and cared for. The two wells on the Rock produced only a brackish, undrinkable water, and the only supply available from Spain was a few barrels brought in by donkey from the Holy Spring beyond San Roque, which was sold to the more prosperous citizens as a special delicacy, to which it was acceptable to add a little whisky. The newly-discovered subterranean lake was not exploited; it formed an emergency reserve. Inside the Rock, distillation plants worked to turn sea water into drinkable fresh water, and they alone would have stood between the Garrison and death by dehydration if the threatened gas attacks had materialized and contaminated the catchments. For our salt sea-water baths we used special cakes of soap, thoughtfully provided by the solicitous Admiralty (and already familiar to us, though not actually used, from our shipwreck rations), but somehow one always ended a bath feeling stickier than ever.

Not only did drinking water have to be found for the almost 30,000 inhabitants of the Rock, but the convoys and their escorts called for water, both those going down the Med and those heading for the Cape. The year that we reached Gib was a dry one, and the water supply gave out. Water had to be sent out from Britain by tanker (a contingency not, of course, known to us at the time).

There was no grass. Garrison sports were played on asphalt and tarmac. The few trees were either naturally drab, like the wild olives, or had become so through a heavy film of dust. As a background colour, green had vanished, to be replaced by grey. And yet, even here, spring worked a miracle. From tiny, seemingly soilless crevasses, wild narcissi bloomed thick and white, scenting all the air of the upper Rock. By April, wild lupins and snapdragons and bright yellow and purple creepers had spread among the stunted olives and myrtle bushes, and in the cultivated public gardens, where cricket was played on a wicket of matting, almonds and oleanders bloomed, and bougain-villea rioted in all its ostentatious puce and magenta.

No food grew on the Rock. As the *Gibraltar Directory and Guide Book* put it, "there is no land suitable for agriculture and animal husbandry; no forests, fisheries or other natural resources". All supplies came in by sea. Fresh milk vanished from our diet, and so did bulky goods, like potatoes. The pre-war source of supply for cattle, poultry and eggs from North Africa had been cut off, and all the horses and mules had been disposed of because of the shortage of cereals on which to feed them. Even the hounds of Calpe Hunt had been destroyed at the start of the war, and rats, mice, apes and foxes were about the only creatures apart from man still living there.

We never felt hungry, but the Americans on the Rock used to worry about vitamin deficiency, and sent home for vitamin pills. They may have been right, as most of us were much less healthy when we left the Rock than when we came, but we never thought of food in medical terms, and swallowing vitamin pills seemed to us hypochondriacal, if not actually effete and decadent.

We might have been more healthy than we were if we had eaten more fruit, of which there was plenty in town, brought from Spain. Peaches, melons, grapes, bananas, pomegranates, oranges and lemons all abounded in the shops, but at prices which made them occasional luxuries to us. A cabbage cost 3s 6d (6d to 8d for a whole two-pound cabbage in England). Perhaps it was the price that prevented

fruit from appearing in the Wrennery except at rare intervals. The Mess funds only ran to sensible suet puddings.

Our pay was quite inadequate to cope with Gibraltar
prices. A small reel of cotton cost 1s, when it was 1d or 2d in
England; a pair of civilian silk stockings cost 25s, well over a
week's pay to us. There was nominal price control, but in
practice it was not enforced. In theory, had one been willing
to do so, one could have reported a trader to the City
Council, but the obstacles were too numerous. To begin
with, it meant obtaining a receipt. The shop never had the
necessary 2d stamp; or else the manager alone was
authorized to issue receipts, but he was out. In the end, if
you wanted the article enough, you paid and said nothing.

Notwithstanding the war, the shops were well supplied
with goods of German and Japanese origin. There were also
exquisitely pretty shoes from Spain, silver filigree and
Spanish Toledo work, and textiles from India. This array of
silk, perfumes and cosmetics (at steep prices, it is true) was
deliberate policy. It was psychological warfare. The
Spaniards who came to work in the dockyard could see, and
take home with them the story, that the beleaguered
garrison was very well off; far better off, in fact, than the
Spaniards themselves. But something had been overlooked,
and it caused a great deal of embarrassment. Nowhere at all
was there any source of sanitary towels. Although for two
years Wrens had been serving on the Rock, no one presumably had faced up to the embarrassment of acquainting
the Admiralty with this delicate problem. We had to write
home and ask our families to keep us supplied by post,
which was very awkward for the few girls who had not got
families. Fortunately, a few months later, Lord Nuffield gave
a sum of money to provide the Women's Services with
extras and luxuries, and this was used by the WRNS to provide us with a free issue. It was a great weight off our minds.

With the coming of war, all Gibraltar's women and
children had been evacuated—some to England, some to the
West Indies. Some 3,000 Gibraltarian men remained, but

fundamentally the Rock had become a vast barracks, containing some 18,000 Servicemen, about 150 Wrens and a handful of Army nurses. To these were added, every day, a ragged horde of about 6,000 cleaners and dock workers pouring across the Isthmus from Spain. The dockyard could not have functioned without them, but streaming in with them came the agents of the German secret service. The Nazis recruited among the Spanish workers, and from time to time saboteurs would be arrested as they were about to blow us all up. Two trials of saboteurs were held during the autumn after our arrival. Two of the accused were executed.

In the late afternoon, armed with the ration of good white propaganda bread which was, to these impoverished Spaniards, one of the main attractions of working in Gibraltar, the horde flowed back into Spain again, and the frontier was closed behind them for the night. After that, the only colours to be seen in the streets of Gibraltar were dark blue, light blue and shades of khaki, plus white in summer when the order went out to the Navy in the Mediterranean to take off serge and put on drill (an order originating, as we understood, in Alexandria, and not always too well suited to the weather in Gib). Homes and hearths were a thing of the past. Until we left the Rock, we should never escape from communal living.

Because Gib was almost exclusively a male community, language was unguarded. The air along Main Street was permanently vibrating with blasphemies and obscenities, until, even if we did not readily fall into the habit of using them ourselves, they seemed a routine and unremarkable part of the environment, which perhaps deprived us of the frisson of excitement with which Britain accommodated itself to the linguistic liberation of later decades. But we were not expected to follow the trend, and indeed the garrison would tenderly protect us from direct assaults of bad language, as distinct from what we casually overheard. Once I was the only girl at a concert during which a sailor stood up and made an intemperate speech, employing a selection of unorthodox words. Someone must have told him there was a Wren in the audience, because afterwards, to my astonishment, he came and apologized to me, saying he had not realized there was a girl present. Women really did, at that time, have a moderating influence.

Inevitably, we were strictly curfewed, and only during daylight hours were we allowed to wander unescorted. If we went out alone or with another girl, as we could during the day, we were the butt of cat-calls, whistles and kissing noises. The Free French matelots and the Spanish dock-workers joined in the game. They did not shout or whistle, but veered unexpectedly towards us in the streets whisper-ing intimately into our ears such mild endearments as "Bonjour cherie", or "Bella—quere compaña?", and other things which we did not understand. It made no difference if you looked like the back of a bus, we all got the same treat-ment, so there was nothing very flattering about it. The barrage persisted even when we were escorted; and our escorts learned to be as deaf as we were to the stream of pleasantries. But an inexperienced escort from a visiting ship could be a serious liability. A gallant, hot-tempered and Spanish-speaking sailor from an American warship once tried to flatten a Spaniard who made a rude remark about the sailor's Wren companion, thinking he would not be understood. Two American Military Policemen quickly intervened, and an 'incident' was averted.

A result of this incessant attention, coupled with the communal living in the Wrennery, was that it was never possible, at any time at all, to be alone. There were times when one needed to go into a corner and cry. There was, after all, a war on, and sometimes bad news came, of families at home killed by bombing; of brothers or fiancés killed in action. One had to get over one's grief in public. Not even the lavatories were entirely private; the doors had wide spaces above them. And we could not step outside the Wrennery without attempts being made to pick us up.

One escape was the rifle range. Rifle shooting made a change from swimming and scrambling over the rocks, but I never developed any skill at it. I hit the outer ring of the target the first time I tried, and there was never any improvement from that point. I tried holding my breath. I tried not holding my breath. Nothing helped. I have a beautiful silver medal inscribed 'Third Prize Gibraltar Rifle Shooting Competition', but only three people entered that particular event.

It was at the range, though, that we used to meet the Dutch. Through Holland and Belgium, across France and into the dry mountains of Spain they came in the night, until at last they reached Gib and volunteered to join up. Most of the escapees were young students. We never asked them about their adventures; there were some questions one did not ask in wartime. All of them, no matter where they came from or in what circumstances, had spent six months in prison in Spain, sometimes in conditions of appalling degradation and brutality. It was such a routine that we concluded there must be an agreement about it between the Spanish authorities and the Nazis, to ensure that all their news would be at least six months out-of-date by the time is reached British Intelligence. Days or even weeks sometimes went by before their passage to England could be assured, and they could unite with their fellow-countrymen already in uniform.

Very firmly not shipped off the Rock were some rather less welcome companions, the Rock 'apes', the tailless Barbary macaques which do not exist anywhere else in Europe apart from zoos. There is a legend that if one does not see a Rock ape within a month of disembarkation, one will die on the Rock. After about a week, we became a little anxious and began to scour the landscape for apes. We need not have worried. It was not long before they joined the party in our Rock-top cabins.

They liked to drop things, to test whether they made the same noise as the thing before, and very soon nothing breakable was left. It was the apes' habit to climb into our sleeping cabin, seize our belongings, in particular mirrors, then sit outside the watch-room on the parapet edging the path that prevented us falling down the precipice, studying themselves in the mirror; then nonchalantly tossing everything down the cliff.

Occasionally the apes joined us in the watch-room, and graciously accepted buns or toffees which they were adept at unwrapping. Sometimes, even under our noses in the watch-room, they stole what was not offered to them. Once an ape seized a bag of sugar buns and made for the door. The owner of the buns gave chase, and the ape dropped them and ran outside. We pushed the door shut and returned to our work.

After a short while there was a slow creaking, the door opened very gradually, and the ape looked slyly round the door at the bag of buns. He was just beginning a stealthy entrance, when the buns' owner turned round, and gave the ape a straight look of unyielding severity, whereupon, like a naughty child that had been caught out, the ape turned and fled.

It had been jocularly noticed, before the war, that the apes would innocently try to tear clothes off lady visitors. This devastating little prank was put down to the assumed attraction that bright clothing must have for the apes. Possibly this record should be amended. We wore naval bell-bottomed trousers and white square-necked sailors' 'flannels' on duty, but the apes' interest in us, rather than in the Seamen, was undeniable. They would sit in a row on the parapet outside the watch-room, gazing intently at us. If we looked up suddenly, they would hastily look away, up at the sky perhaps, with an expression on their faces as if they were trying to whistle a careless little tune.

Their society was highly organized. The leader was Scruffy, but a little before Christmas 1943 Scruffy disappeared, and Adonis took over the leadership. *The Times* of London reported that Scruffy's body had been seen floating in the Bay, but this report proved premature, and only served to spread alarm and despondency among Scruffy's supporters quite unnecessarily. Early in the New Year Scruffy reappeared, fought it out with Adonis, and re-established his supremacy. When at last he died, full of years and honour, he was eighteen, the longest-lived ape in the records.

The records are carefully kept. As everyone knows, British power over Gibraltar will last as long as the apes are there, and no longer. A highly solicitous eye is kept on ape welfare. Historically, it was usually the Army that had the responsibility, providing two regular meals a day up at the top of the Rock. Births and deaths were published in the Fortress orders, and all apes named. Even so, numbers had declined lamentably, and by the mid-1940s a signal was received from Churchill himself stating that 'the ape pack will be maintained'. Some new blood was introduced from Spanish Morocco, where the Spanish army, gaily disregarding the legend, kindly cooperated by catching the apes. Perhaps they were not all that anxious to change places with the British Garrison.

Chapter VIII

Social Butterflies

Socially speaking, we got off to a slow start. For obvious reasons, we were not allowed outside the Wrennery after 8 p.m. without a male escort, and as we did not know anyone, we had perforce to remain rather disconsolately all evening behind the chicken wire round our huts, patio prisoners gazing enviously at the girls who had escorts and could set foot outside the Wrennery.

This phase did not last. Invitations to dances and parties came in to the Wrennery at the rate of three or four a week. Usually these were general invitations from sergeants' Messes, but sometimes there would be a more specific invitation. *Warspite*, for instance, came in to Gib and the communications ratings invited twelve of the WRNS communications ratings to go aboard. Invitations to visit ships were always popular. We had never, as telegraphists, been stationed within reach of the real sea-going Navy, and it rejoiced our hearts to see the great ships in the harbour. *Warspite* remained at Gib for a long time. She had been hit by a radio-controlled bomb off Salerno, and there was work to be done on her, so she became a familiar sight in the dockyard. The Royal Artillery Band used to give concerts aboard her.

One of our first visits was to the wardroom of a visiting corvette, officered entirely by the RNVR. Three or four years previously every one of those officers had been in banks or insurance offices; now they were in sole charge of a fighting ship sailing the seven seas. It made our responsibilities at our wireless sets look rather insignificant.

We learnt later on a little of what it felt like to go to sea in a small naval vessel. A minelayer called *HMS Linnet* took us for a day's cruise in the Bay and the Straits, and we took turns standing duty at the wheel with a strong Seaman to help us when the winds and waves threatened to chase us off course. It was a boisterous March day, and keeping one's eyes fixed on the compass needle did nothing to alleviate incipient sea-sickness, but a Chief Petty Officer fed us draughts of orange liqueur all day, and this kept us on our feet.

Another great battleship to visit Gib was the *USS Texas.* She sent several quarts of ice-cream and four wedding dresses up to the Wrennery, but did not stay in port long enough to see the dresses used. There were occasional weddings on the Rock, but very few. Most people felt they needed to assess their feelings in a more normal atmosphere than Gibraltar before taking the irrevocable (as we then thought of it) step of getting hitched.

There had been some discussion in Parliament as to the wisdom, even the justification, for sending young Service women into the moral hazard of service abroad. Overseas, as our superintendent at the Drafting Depot had warned us, was distinctly Romantic, at least potentially. The climate was languorous, alcohol plentiful (which was not often the case at home), and because there were so few of us, we were all treated as eminently desirable. We were outnumbered by about 200 to one.

And yet, in an era when contraceptives for single women were extremely hard to obtain and abortions out of the question, very few Wrens had to put the WRNS to the trouble of shipping them home early. Most of us in those days were sincere church-going Christians, intending to wait for Mr. Right before we lost our virginity. The few tragedies (as they then were, for the accepted wisdom of the time was that an unmarried mother would almost certainly have to be parted from her baby), were usually the result of genuine love affairs rather than casual promiscuity. In a community like Gib it was hard to find out whether a man was married or not unless he chose to be frank about it, and one girl sent home was actually officially engaged to the father of her baby, who had neglected to mention that he was already married.

Despite the attention we got, not many of the British Servicemen we met seemed really to believe that we were there 'for one purpose and one purpose only'. The Americans, however, did tend to assume that our work at code books and wireless sets and teleprinters was only a blind for our main usefulness, and one or two American parties broke up in disorder, the Wrens involved returning to the Wrennery in high dudgeon.

Still, there was no denying that from the point of view of Finding Romance, things looked very promising. It was all the more disquieting therefore to find a subtle change coming over our attitude towards the opposite sex. The eternal round of parties in unattractive Mess halls with floors awash with spilt beer was losing its appeal. Besides, our hosts were usually NCOs much older than we were, who clumped unmercifully on our feet, saying merrily "I am enjoying this! I haven't danced for two years!" It became a stock phrase, like "Do you come here often?" Rather wistfully we wondered if the officers' parties were any more glamorous or—not to put too fine a point on it—romantic; but we had no chance to find out. As watch-keepers, half our evenings were spent on top of the Rock, and though officers' Messes sent invitations to the Wrennery, by sheer chance our watch was on duty for every such dance for four months on end, so our evening dresses remained scrumpled up in our kit-bags.

After a while we realized that we would just as soon sit in the fo'c's'le as go to any more parties. But we felt we ought to go. If the Wrens did not go to the parties, there was no one else who could, and perhaps we ought to accept some responsibility for trying to sustain garrison morale. Wearily we put on the civilian cotton frocks we had bought with our coupons in London, and set out determined to be bright and gay* and good company. Wearily we came back at curfew time and nursed our bruised feet.

"I wonder", said one of the Wrens, "if the position were reversed, how many of these men would turn out to rescue us from being wall-flowers?"

We agreed that of course none would. We decided that on the whole we hated men. We should like to go out for the evening for a quiet, relaxed uncomplicated visit to the cinema with a girl friend. But it was impossible, and would remain so until we left the Rock.

Except on Saturday nights, there was nowhere in the Wrennery to which we could invite men after 6 p.m., and nowhere to which they could invite us unless they belonged to some privileged Mess. Strolling about in the dark with a male companion invited the wrong kind of attention … so where was one to go?

Going out to eat and drink was complicated and depended on the rank of one's escort. The two best hotels, at one of which there was dancing, were reserved for officers only. The third hotel supposedly served the lower deck, but in practice usually made some excuse not to do so. The fourth was a large gloomy restaurant, so expensive that it cost a rating about half a week's pay to take a girl there. There was no canteen, not even a YMCA, on the Rock, though one was being built and was opened about a year before the end of the war.

There was a yacht club — reserved for officers. There was a library — reserved for officers.

---

* 'Gay' at the time implied light-hearted, cheerful, merry, brightly dressed, good company. A secondary meaning of 'immoral' was described in the dictionary as being somewhat archaic and not commonly imputed. Intimations of homosexuality were limited to very restricted circles.

The answer was to go to the cinema. In fact, there was almost nothing else to do. The projectors were a little uncertain, we might see the same news reel for five or six weeks running, and it was wise to hunt under the arms of the seat for bugs before sitting down, but apart from that we spent many happy hours in the cinema. It was not unusual to be the only girl in the audience. On one occasion I was the only female at a cinema showing *The Gentle Sex,* a film about the ATS. In the film, a Scottish ATS girl, commiserating with another who is cold, offers to lend her her 'spencers'. I laughed, but no one else did, and from all over the cinema I heard the murmur go up, "What are spencers?" Messages requesting elucidation were passed along the row to me. (In case anyone is still wondering, a spencer is a woolly under-bodice, and it's worn for warmth, not glamour.)

For ratings there was a series of liquor dives along Main Street, into which it was impossible to take a girl. Even to walk along Main Street at night was hazardous, for drunk but cheerful Servicemen would be lined up urinating in the gutter with merry shouts of "Hullo Jenny" if a startled Wren and her escort attempted to go home that way. There was a less direct route back to the Wrennery, and we learnt to take it. Ultimately Main Street was put out of bounds to Wrens at night.

In these conditions, it was not surprising that many of the Wrens became avid pip-hunters. We had a not wholly undeserved reputation for being snobs. But nothing we did could please everyone. If we walked along the street with a sailor, the other Services shouted, "What's wrong with the Army?" (or Air Force, if they were airmen, but it was the Army that did most of the shouting). If we were with an NCO they shouted that we were stuck up; if we were with an officer they shouted, though from a safer distance, that we were snobs; if we went out with an American, we were greeted with a non-stop chorus of "What's wrong with the British?"

The perpetual disparity between commissioned and non-commissioned amenities led to discontent. One outlet was the Garrison Literary and Debating Society, in which Other Ranks were permitted to use the Library facilities for its meetings. Back in Scarborough days we had boasted a couple of Wren Communists, middle-class girls who defied the bourgeoisie by standing up in the fo'c's'le every now and then and singing the Red Flag. It is difficult to be a rebel against society when one belongs to a uniformed and disciplined Service, and the only outlet this couple could find was to wash their hair less frequently than the rest of us, which caused most of us to identify Communism with lack of personal hygiene and find it unattractive in consequence. The Rock Communists were much the same. They wore their hair longer than I could have believed Army regulations allowed, and exuded a personal repulsiveness which made it difficult to warm to their cause. They gave me copies of *The Daily Worker* to read, but I was soon prejudiced against it by what I considered its bad manners. I was completely ignorant of the tenets of Marxism, which, not having been explored by Xenophon, Virgil, or I.A. Richards, had been left out of my education. My antipathy to Communism was even less intelligently based than was my comrades' sympathy.

Lively debates proceeded however on such topics as 'The world is in more need of a moral than an economic revolution', and 'This house views with apprehension the increasing activities of women outside the home..' To my surprise, the Servicemen rejected the second proposition, not entirely, I think, out of admiration for the New Soviet Woman. And shortly afterwards an RAF debating society voted for 'Equal Pay for Equal Work'. Some sort of yeast seemed to be at work among the Servicemen. No longer were their women's interests supposed to be exclusively confined to the kitchen sink.

Other tensions were less readily dispelled. When we landed in early August, the Italians were our enemies. A month later they were our former enemies, and six weeks after that they declared war on Germany, and became our gallant allies; and units of their Navy visited Gibraltar. British Seamen were supposed to salute allied officers, but they were entirely unwilling to accord Marks of Respect to Italian officers within six weeks of being at war with them, and as for the Free French, they continued to fight the Italians at every opportunity, no matter what the odds, on the streets of Gibraltar; fights in which the British enthusiastically breathed life into the Entente Cordiale and helped the French. After a number of Italians had to be fished out of the harbour, wet, bruised and humiliated, all Italians were confined to their ships after 4 p.m.

Once a fight started, it spread rapidly. There was a restlessness abroad, people were bored and felt restricted. On one occasion a group of sailors and Wrens from our station went to a dance in town. I had to go back up the Rock for the night watch and when curfew time approached and the other Wrens went back to the Wrennery I left the dance hall to find the transport, escorted by a quiet and sober young sailor named Geoff, who was due on the same night watch that I was. Outside the hall, a drunk sailor, also from our station, came up, hung on to me and said he would see me to the car. At that moment a Leading Seaman joined us, and shrewdly pulled rank, saying he would settle the question of which sailor took the Wren to the car. A quick, melting escape along the pavement was impossible, as it was jammed solid with sailors, so I silently blessed the Leading Seaman for taking charge of the situation. He was spinning a coin and would obviously see to it that the drunk lost the toss.

Unfortunately, the Leading Seaman was drunk too, and made the drunk win the toss. A second sober Seaman, seeing me in difficulty, pushed his way through to help Geoff rescue me, but the drunk hit him. It was the signal for a general set-to. Every Seaman in sight punched the Seaman next to him. The road and the pavement were completely filled with fighting men, and Geoff and I could not move.

As the fighting surged round me, a third sailor set out to rescue me. He was a small, cheerful little soul with fair curly hair and blue eyes. He had a cherubic face and a satanic disposition, and used to sit next to me on watch confiding to me how much he hated what he called 'po' music, and persuading flies to walk down a paper chute which he had constructed, and then guillotining them with a razor blade as they emerged. He now decided that, as in a fire, the air is clearest at ground level, so he crawled through the mêlée and emerged just above ground level over to the right, his hat well back on his fair curls, and a finger crooked to beckon me.

"This way," he called, "this way, Miss Jones".

Why he used my surname I don't know, no one else did, and it was only an approximation of my name anyway, but the formality added a final absurdity to the whole situation. Before I had time to respond, stamping, shuffling feet closed in front of his head, and he vanished behind them.

Undeterred, he next popped through, still at ground level, somewhere on my left. He still had his hat on, and his finger still beckoned confidently.

"This way!" he called, but got no further. A wave of navy blue rolled over him.

Shortly after that the Army got involved, and the street became fuller than ever. Then whistles blew and the Military Police came into the street from one end, the naval picket from the other. In the breathing space that followed Geoff and I got away to the car. Social problems had become quite impossibly complex since the days when I had worried about how to hold a cocktail glass.

Another activity in which we could indulge was music. Gibraltar Anglican Cathedral asked for volunteers to perform Handel's *Messiah* at Christmas 1943. It was an unusual choir, there were three or four tenors and basses for every soprano and also, since we worked watches, not more than half the handful of Wrens were ever there together until the final performances. Our untrained throats felt the strain. I developed a longing for Allen and Hanbury's blackcurrant throat pastilles. I went to the 'English Chemist', a very hushed and professional establishment with big coloured bottles in its brass-edged window.

"I want some throat pastilles", I said. "Have you Allen and Hanbury's?"

The chemist looked at me severely.

"Do you want throat pastilles?" he said. "Or do you want sweets?"

I was so abashed that I said I wanted throat pastilles, whereupon he sold me some utterly revolting concoctions, which I gave to the cockroaches. The next chemist was less severe. He had no Allen and Hanbury's but he had some other blackcurrant pastilles. He persuaded me to buy them, but I did not like them very much. The third time I set out to buy my throat pastilles I vowed I would not be persuaded to take any others.

"Have you any Allen and Hanbury's blackcurrant throat pastilles?" I asked chemist number three.

"No," he said, "but I have Parke Davis."

"No thank you", I said, and turned to go.

There was a little American sailor sitting on a stool at the counter. He jumped up.

"Pardon me," he said, "but Parke Davis are quite the best."

"Well, but you see ..." I began.

"I worked for them back in the States," continued the little sailor, "I know. They're quite the best."

I bought a packet of Parke Davis throat pastilles. It seemed rude not to. As I was leaving, I remembered another commodity for which I had been searching.

"By the way," I said, "have you any shampoo?"

"No. I don't think you'll find any anywhere on the Rock", said the chemist.

The little sailor jumped up again.

"We've plenty at our base", he said.

"Where is your base?" I asked. I thought perhaps there was an American PX store, and that they would let me buy some shampoo.

"Dakar, West Africa."

My hopes collapsed. There was no prospect of my popping to Dakar on a shopping spree.

"We'll send some along", said the sailor. "We're pharmacists' mates, and we're always writing up to this drug store. You leave your name here, and he'll tell you when it comes in."

I thanked him.

"That's OK", he said. "The British have done us a good turn a day since we've been with them, and if we can do anything for you, we'll be delighted."

About two weeks later the chemist phoned me to say that three bottles of Fitch's shampoo had been flown in from Dakar. But that was not the end of the story.

Something went wrong with the Christmas mail for Gib that year. Air letters came in, but all the Christmas surface mail went astray, and did not arrive until some weeks after Christmas. So no one had any Christmas presents.

But on Christmas Eve the chemist phoned again to say that another parcel had arrived by air from Dakar. I collected the parcel, and in it was a magnificent cross-section of the Dakar PX store. There were three more bottles of shampoo, four tablets of soap, a tin of peanuts, ten bars of chocolate, various packets of toffees and liquorice sweets, and twenty different kinds of chewing gum. The whole cabin unpacked and repacked this parcel in turn, and we all shared in the contents. It was the only Christmas parcel any of us had.

Perhaps the storm that Christmas had something to do with the delay in our mail. It became a legend. At the southern end of the Rock the spray was carrying almost from sea to sea. Shut inside the cathedral, we ploughed our earnest way through the *Messiah* and the young airman from North Front Air Station filled the vaults with 'Why do the heathen so furiously rage together?' in a rich and liquid bass, as strong and unruly as the wind that howled outside. Radio Gibraltar broadcast us to the ships tossing out at sea, and almost two thousand people came to the cathedral to hear us sing, remembering, perhaps, the Choral Society in the civic hall at home, where, in the cities and towns across Britain, amateur *Messiah*s were heralding Christmas.

Chapter IX

Dwindling Duties

At Scarborough we had worked very hard, and expected, indeed were only too willing, to do so again. But Italy had dropped out of the war within barely a month of our arrival in the Mediterranean, and life at our wireless station quietened down. Even before Christmas, drafts of sailors were beginning to leave, some going down the Med to Malta or Alexandria, some home to Britain to retrain for the Far East.

With Italian martial activity completely scaled down, and German U-boats, though still operating in the Med, seemingly much less intensively, we spent a good deal of our time searching for blockade runners. Any neutral shipping which was plotted far from the trade routes prescribed by the Allies was considered suspicious, and worthy of investigation. This meant working on international frequencies, and learning a new form of 'operators' chat', known as the international E-code. On one occasion, so we were told, an offending vessel laden with Chanel No. 5 had been brought into Gib harbour. The sailors began to make jubilant mention of the Prize money that would be distributed to the Navy at the end of the war. Wrens did not qualify for Prize money, but for a few days we hoped that one or two bottles of perfume would find their way to us. We were to be disappointed.

Once, searching the international wave bands rather aimlessly, I heard a tremulous little transmitter urgently calling anyone who would listen. Some hours later the squeaky little calls were still being made, and at last Geneva Radio replied, whereupon the caller signalled "Ici, Yougoslavie Libre". Somewhere in the hills beyond the Adriatic the partisans were trying to contact the outside world. It was interesting, but not our job.

No replacements came to replace the departing drafts of sailors. Our numbers dwindled, and we felt useless, leaves eddying in a backwater while the main torrent of the war passed us by. We were good telegraphists, we had worked hard to acquire the skills that we were not now being called upon to use. It was Rachel who summed up our frustration:

> So don't get any wrong ideas
> When you leave home as volunteers;
> We wanted to help to win the war,
> But we should have thought of that before.
> They don't want operators wise,
> They just want social butterflies.

Our morale was being assailed from other quarters, too. For one thing, there were the bedbugs. Our sleeping cabin was infested with them, and we could not fumigate the room because of the electrical installations with which we shared it. Our bedding was stored in a wooden cupboard, clearly infested, which we burnt. We sent the bedclothes for fumigation. We lived in a perpetual mist of fine white insecticide powder. It made no difference. The bugs loved the powder, and throve exceedingly. Havoc said that after a few months we should probably become immune to their bites, so we just had to live in hope, and after a while we did seem to suffer less.

There was another possible reason for the improvement, and that was that we managed to get the pallets replaced with beds, proper beds, instead of wooden pallets. The reason for this was that we nearly mutinied over the rats. They had bodies a foot long, plus another twelve inches of tail. Mice we were quite fond of, and we shared our hut down in the town with a pleasant, woofly-nosed little family which used to come in on rainy days. But the rats were another matter. The rats were insolent and completely unafraid, even in daylight. They had no trouble in running over our flat pallets, and we urgently requested beds in the mistaken belief that perhaps the rats would not bother to jump up so high. The request was approved, and we waited expectantly, but no action was taken, and some weeks later, after some particularly unpleasant encounters including Sheila being woken on her pallet by a rat chewing her hair, we marched in a not very orderly fashion to see our First Officer, and announced (technically mutiny I suppose) that we were not returning to work until we had got beds. She was astonished that nothing had been done, and we got the beds quite quickly.

The sailors were as frightened of the rats as we were, so we felt that it was not just feminine silliness. Once, a sailor who had gone off to make tea came hurrying back into the watch-room shouting, "Quick! A broom! There's a rat in the office!" He seized a broom and rushed out again, and the charge-hand eyed his vanishing figure lugubriously.

"We shall see", he said, "which of them comes back and puts the headphones on."

The rat menace on the Rock grew so serious that finally, in 1945, an all-out Combined Services operation was initiated against them. The Gibraltar Directory speaks rather proudly of this campaign, but it came too late to save us. Left to ourselves, we were never very effective against the rats.

If it wasn't the rats and the bugs disturbing our sleep, it was the electrical equipment. The noise it made, coupled with vivid bursts of Morse through the thin Nissen partition that separated us from the nearest watch-room, made sleep difficult between watches. Also, even without the stress of being subjected to fumigation, the equipment proved delicate, and broke down from time to time, and then the off-duty watch would be woken by an invasion of sailors trying to put it right. These eruptions of sailors into our bedroom could have been embarrassing, considering that we were the only women in their lives at the time, but the proprieties were scrupulously observed, and, under the guidance of a Chief Petty Officer telegraphist, the sailors would pretend that they did not know we were there, and we would pretend to be asleep. There were no embarrassing incidents at all. But perhaps, what with our bug bites, we were just too repulsive.

Lack of sleep was becoming a problem. We would descend to the Wrennery for our twenty-four hours off-duty, and if we were coming off the midnight-to-0800 watch, our first need would be to sleep. But this was almost as difficult in the Wrennery as up at the wireless station. We shared our hut with six day workers, and day workers never really learnt that watch-keepers needed to sleep during the day. The last of the day workers pottered out to her job of sorting out ball bearings at the Gunnery School at about half past ten. The Fleet Mail clerks were the first to return for lunch, full of song, merriment, and pineapples from the Azores (they were always getting presents from visiting ships), at about noon. Bursting open the door of our hut, they would see us in bed, suddenly remember about watch-keeping, and noisily hush one another. But by then it was too late, we would be awake, and the broiling noon heat of our iron-roofed huts would be too intense for us to fall asleep again.

As the weeks wore on, we realized that somehow we must learn to manage without sleep. Night watches at the station became an agony of trying to stay awake. I took up smoking, which had two advantages: by saying 'in 15 minutes I shall have a cigarette' it helped one to stay awake while watching the minutes tick by; and once the cigarette was lit, there was always the hope of burning oneself if one began to fall asleep. Thus began a habit I was not to break for thirty years. One horrendous night I did drowse off. Fortunately, the charge-hand saw my head nod, immediately tuned in to my frequency, and picked up a U-boat—or anyway, he told me he did. It was utterly humiliating, and a reminder that on our job a moment's inattention could be deeply damaging.

But something happened to cheer us all up. An agreement was reached with Spain which permitted Other Ranks wearing civilian clothes to cross the border and visit Spain (officers were already allowed to go to Spain for the day, but the concession had not extended to ORs.) Numbers were strictly limited. Six Wrens per week were to be allowed over, which meant that our turn would come about once in six months. We could not actually go on leave, but only pop over between watches. Petty Officers and above could go across the isthmus to La Linea, but Leading Hands and below could go only to Algeciras across the Bay. Since it was impossible to leave Gib by road except by crossing the isthmus into La Linea, those of us who were not Petty Officers had to leave by sea, and there was only one way to do that: to take the ferry across the Bay. It left at 10.30 a.m., deposited passengers in Algeciras at 11 a.m., and the last ferry back was at 3 p.m., so permission to visit Spain therefore turned out, in practice, to allow four hours in Spain every six months. We could not, after all, walk off the Rock in the early morning on a free day and spend all day exultantly walking into the hills, nor could we go to a bullfight, as they were held late in the day, when the heat was past its worst; nor could we sit in Spanish cafés, sipping an evening aperitif and ordering dinner.

This brought up a very sore point. Not only were we not Petty Officers, we had not even become Leading Wrens, though we had confidently expected our promotion, based on the exams we had done at Scarborough, to be waiting for us when we reached Gib. When several months had passed, and those we had left behind in England had been rated up, we asked for enquiries to be made. A reply came back that the question of promoting Wren telegraphists in Gibraltar did not arise, as there were no Wren telegraphists in Gibraltar. It was as we suspected. Officially, we had ceased to exist. A further deterioration in our morale set in, and our patriotic poems became tinged with a vein of cynicism.

The months passed, signals flew to and fro, Admiralty Fleet Orders were consulted to determine whether, now that we had no vast watch for which to be responsible, we could all be promoted. Oracles replied that Wrens abroad were promoted from their home rosters, so that service abroad could not cause cancellation of a promotion earned at home. But nothing happened. Those in England who had been on the training course after us, and were therefore about six months our juniors, had been Leading Wrens for some time, and were training to be Petty Officers. For us, it seemed, the future held nothing but the ultimate disgrace of having to put up three-year good conduct badges with no emblem of promotion above them—a public admission that one was considered Well-intentioned but Thick.

"How are we ever going to get jobs after the war?" I lamented to Duncan. "It's not as if we've got an excuse, like the prisoners of war. We shan't be considered fit for anything but scrubbing."

"You'll just have to stay in the Navy, then, won't you?" said Duncan.

"I don't care two bloody hoots about the Navy", I said.

Duncan was shocked. He had never heard me swear before. I was appalled, not so much at my language as at my sentiments. Surely it wasn't true? I lifted my eyes from the rock on which we were sitting and looked at the big grey ships in the harbour, and I knew it was not true.

Duncan was my constant companion. He was twenty-four. He was six feet tall (well, almost), he had thick brown hair and gentle hazel eyes, straight eyebrows, a straight nose, a slow rather quizzical smile and soft Scottish voice. He was hopeless at dancing, but I liked him all the same.

He was a leading telegraphist (though not at our station), and a peace-time sailor. He had joined the Navy at seventeen, and had spent his time with the Home Fleet until the war, and then had been on the Malta convoys until he was sent to Gib. He had no relations. He had been looked after, as a baby, by foster parents in the Scottish lowlands, but they had died when he was twelve, and he had left school to go to work as a gamekeeper's assistant. He was still much of a country boy, knowledgeable about the flowers that grew wild on the Rock, recognizing the scent where a fox had passed among the stunted trees.

Our backgrounds held nothing in common at all. Furthermore, he was a Roman Catholic. He told me this quite suddenly three months after we met, in the middle of a film show of *My Sister Eileen*. As I could think of nothing to say in reply I went on looking at the screen. A Roman Catholic! But my family would never stand for … come to that, neither would I.

Then I realized that I had caught myself red-handed. Men complained that you only had to ask a girl out a few times and she started hearing wedding bells, and I had fallen into just that trap. Differences of religious belief were important only if people were thinking of getting married, they did not matter at all between friends. And we were simply friends.

We became inseparable. I went and cheered the football matches in which he played, and he came to hear the choir in which I sang. Though he had so little formal education, he liked to read and to talk over his books with me. And I liked to be with him because he was sane and gentle and genuine, and never let difficulties get him down as I did. We signed on to learn Spanish together in the dockyard school. Spanish gave me little trouble; I knew Latin well, and French fairly well. But for Duncan, it was a struggle. Book learning did not come easily to him.

When our Spanish had become fairly proficient, we requested permission to go to Spain. Valid smallpox vaccination certificates were a condition of entry, which gave me a problem because of the failure of my attempt to get vaccinated in Scarborough, and it took three further efforts in Gib before it was decided that a little flake of skin at the site where my three new attempts had been made was proof enough that I had 'taken'.

Many a Wren had been sadly disillusioned when her escort turned up for the trip in dull civilian clothes and the glamour of a uniform was gone. Duncan, however, looked more handsome than ever. But Algeciras was a shock. It had been bombed. We had forgotten that neutral Spain, too, had been at war. Algeciras was the first town attacked by Franco's troops when they came over from North Africa. Even now, five years after the end of their war, the town swarmed with Nationalist troops, their khaki greatcoats ankle-length like the Germans. Unlike the Germans, they wore a frivolous red tassel down the front of their caps.

There was nothing frivolous-looking about the arms they carried. Rifles and belts of ammunition seemed to be a permanent feature of their equipment. We were more than a little intimidated, and began to think that possibly the Rock was the more relaxed place after all. Cautiously we admired the blue mosaics of the huge fountain in the town square, surrounded by neat palms and decorative orange trees in full fruit. Everywhere the Moorish passion for mosaics obtruded, even to the lines of blue and white tiles enclosing the dry empty flower beds.

All of us who went to Algeciras had one ambition: to eat our lunch at the Hotel Reina Cristina. We were allowed to take £1 with us, and the lunch would cost us about 15s, but to live in style for just one hour would be well worth the cost. Besides, the Reina Cristina was supposed to be full of blond Teutonic agents, their spy glasses trained on Gibraltar, their iron crosses clinking on their chests. We wanted to see them at work, racing from the terrace that looked across the blissful expanse of water now separating us from our prison home to the telephones where they would report direct to Berlin the latest movements of shipping in the harbour.

But there were no very obvious agents on the hotel terrace. So we went to lunch, and had fried octopus, and waffles with maple syrup. That was all there was time for before the ferry went back.

We had one other chance to go to Spain, so we savoured the forgotten delight of walking more than two miles in the same direction. Britons were not encouraged to wander in the Spanish countryside, for fear of stumbling upon secret Spanish defences, but the Algeciras Office of Information assured us that if we walked along the main road we should not be arrested. So we took the Malaga-Cadiz road, and walked gladly in the noon-day heat.

There were strange sights waiting for a Rockite. There were children learning their lessons in the fields — we never saw children in Gibraltar. There was green wheat springing, fine horses being brought down from the hills by the Spanish army, and ahead of us a road that ran free, free, free to the distant hills.

We could not go far, the three o'clock deadline of the waiting ferry remained. Instead of the exotic food and polished spaciousness of the Reina Cristina, we had eggs fried in oil on the veranda of a country inn, where the wooden tables and chairs were scrubbed white in the sun, and swallows flew to and fro under the eaves. No one else was there, no one to whistle or catcall, no one to look at a sailor's uniform and say they were sorry, but the table was reserved. Gib and its little miseries were far away and very, very unimportant.

Duncan was made a Petty Officer, and we were able to spend time in the PO's Mess at his wireless station. Our off-duty hours became quite civilized; for instance, there were table-cloths in the PO's Mess. Most of the Petty Officers were pre-war sailors, and in the evenings, over a game of cards or a mug of beer or thick naval cocoa, they would reminisce about the Home Fleet before the war — the time the Fleet went to Lisbon and eight sailors licked fourteen Portuguese; the day they heard that *Thetis* was on the bottom, and raced to Liverpool Bay in a doomed attempt to save her crew; the day Lord Louis came aboard ... conversation, especially in a telegraphist Mess, never seemed to go on for long without Lord Louis being mentioned.

One day we had a visitor, a Chief Petty Officer from the Trawler Base.

"It was when I was on the China Station", he began. "We'd got some of the boys painting the side, down on bosun's chairs they were. There were sharks in them seas, and the Duty Officer had told off some of the lads as look-outs, in case any of the boys pitched in.

"Well, stand-easy went, and one of these look-outs reckoned he could nip down for a quick mug of cocoa and no one would be any the wiser. When he gets back up again, his lad's vanished. No one on the bosun's chair, nothing but a cap, see, floating away on the tide. There were sharks, mind, in them waters.

"So he gives the alarm, man overboard. They get the boat away, and they row after the cap. Never got it though — tide was going too fast.

"Well, after a bit they stop rowing for a look around and the chap in the bow says 'who're we looking for?' The fellow in front of him turns round, takes a look at him, and says 'You'.

"He'd heard them pipe stand-easy, see, and he'd nipped in through a port-hole for his cocoa. Next he knew, it was 'boat's crew away', so he'd gone, he was boat's crew that day. Things like that, they was always happening on the China Station. I remember the time ..."

There was always someone with a tale to tell in the PO's Mess. And they were independent men, those Royal Navy Petty Officers. There was some talk in the papers at the time of establishing a hostel in London for Seamen in transit.

"Spoon feeding", said the POs. "Since when has a Navy man not been able to make his own way through London?"

"Since the HOs came in", said someone else. The 'HOs' were the men who had joined, like me, for 'Hostilities Only'.

I was reminded of them a year later, when an ex-Navy CPO was instructing us in technical electricity.

"Family allowance!" he snorted (the Beveridge Report was being hotly debated at the time). "What bloody business of the Government is it how many children I'll have? I know what I earn; it's up to me to decide what family I can afford."

Once there was a rather different evening. The Thursday Club, the RAF's debating society, held a dinner, and four Wrens who had from time to time taken part in their debates were invited. I was placed next to an Army captain, a dark young man with an intense, angular face. He told me that before the war he had been at Oxford reading law. I told him about the place at Lady Margaret Hall that I had relinquished.

"You must go back," he said. "Move heaven and earth to go back. Oxford is Paradise."

The sharp edges of his features seemed to soften; he smiled into the distance, across the trestle tables, and the hundred ravenous airmen.

"Whenever I feel depressed, or think that life is not worth living, I remember Oxford", he said. "I was up for four years. They were the most wonderful years of my life. All summer on the river; take your books and punt on the Isis, browse and read in the sun. And the Commem. Balls! Lovely dresses ... champagne all night long, and then in the morning you go back to the river and punt upstream for breakfast at the pub ... sit in the garden in your evening dress and have bacon and eggs and coffee. May morning ... everyone gets up at dawn, and you go down to Magdalene Bridge and the choir sings from the tower at sunrise ... And the people! Wonderful people! The most interesting people in the world are at Oxford. You go to parties, and you meet everybody, talk all night. Oxford is heaven."

I looked at the young captain. Perhaps there was something in what he said. I particularly liked the bit about the champagne and the ball dresses; I was so tired of beer and blue serge.

My companion emerged from his reverie and spoke sharply.

"I know what it will be," he said, "you'll have to choose between Oxford and wedding bells. Well, all I can say is, if you choose wedding bells, make sure it's someone who will bring into your life something of what you will miss if you don't go to Oxford."

Suddenly I did not want to talk to the Army captain any more. There was something in the future that I did not want to face.

But what to do after the war was a distant problem. There was still a war to be won; only we were doing practically nothing about it. Most of our friends, including Joy, had gone to Colombo, and were pursuing the war in the Far East. A few, like Gay, were still in England. All our contemporaries were Leading Wrens, only we, languishing on the Rock, were forgotten.

At last, nearly a year after our first leading rate exam, we received word that there was no record of our ever having taken any exams. We should have to start again, but if we confirmed our claim by passing the exam, we should be given the same seniority as our contemporaries in Colombo.

The syllabus had been changed again, so lectures were arranged for us, and all our mornings off watch were devoted to study. There was less W/T procedure than before, but more technical material of the type that some of us had studied over a year earlier when we went to night school at the Technical College in Scarborough. We filled up notebooks with drawings of batteries and accumulators and Memorable Points written in capitals, such as ANY SEDIMENT OTHER THAN BROWN (LEAD PEROXIDE) INDICATES WRONG TREATMENT. For the third time we sat our leading rate exams.

We were becoming what the Navy calls 'chokka'. We were fed up with bugs and rats and feeling useless and getting very little sleep and no promotion. We were rapidly becoming (another piece of naval jargon) 'stroppy', inclined to uncooperativeness bordering on insolence, a bias against all in authority that not even Duncan's influence could mitigate. Our immediate superiors were sympathetic, but somewhere in the labyrinthine corridors of Admiralty were

'They'. They were nameless and faceless. We did not know if they were men or women, we only knew that without Their cooperation we were helpless, and They, far from cooperating, seemed to lose every piece of paper referring to us. Were we in the waste-paper basket? The in-tray? Under the blotting paper? Had we yet established to their satisfaction that we existed?

Apparently not. There being virtually nothing for us to do, we started hopefully on the Petty Officer's course, for which we were more than eligible if we got our promised seniority. We spent our mornings puzzling over Resistances in Parallel and the Admiralty Handbook of Wireless Telegraphy.

Two months later our work as telegraphists came to an indisputable end. There was unquestionably nothing whatever for us to do. The last sailors left and went down the Mediterranean. We hoped to follow them to Alexandria, but instead it was decided to send us to the UK to do the Petty Officer's course and retrain for the Japanese war. The only snag was that our third set of exam papers had apparently passed into limbo. There had been no response, and even now we were not Leading Wrens.

It came to the ears of the Admiral that he had a round dozen Wrens fuming with rage at the top of the Rock. No doubt he had many more important things to do, but he sent for us, and listened to our song of woe. Then he sent a stiff signal, and we were rated up by return of post—but not, as we had fondly imagined, from the date on which our friends at home had been promoted, not even from the date on which, for the third time, we had passed the exam; but from the date of the Admiral's signal.

Our draft abroad had cost us a year's seniority. Five of us, girls from sheltered, cocooned families, had not known till then that the world does not always pay 20s in the £. But Havoc knew. Havoc had always known. We did report to Slops (the Naval clothing stores) to pick up the blue anchor badges which our new status entitled us to sew on our left arms, but they had none.

There was an aircraft carrier in the harbour, *HMS Ravager*. We were told to pack our kit-bags and report aboard her at 1300 hours on 27th June.

Every penny we possessed was spent buying things for our oppressed civilian relatives at home. Yards of silk were crammed into our suitcases, with packets of dried fruit; odd corners were stuffed with lemons and oranges, bananas bulged from the top of our kit-bags. Each of us, with our thirsty fathers in mind, was anxiously selecting bottles of Spanish sherry and counting how much we could afford to put down on gin.

Our luggage had multiplied since we arrived. For one thing, we had been asking all year for every stitch of civilian clothing our families could send us, and in my case even the old family dressing-up box had been rifled and hopeful contents sent out to me to be turned into contemporary civilian wear. We begged, borrowed or stole extra crates and suitcases.

It was Duncan who organized my packing, who tied up my gramophone records with the laces from his football boots, nailed up the crate of sherry for my father, supplied us all with ropes to secure our bulging cases.

Before we left, we held a party. Duncan came in his Number Six suit, the magnificent tropical shore dress of the peace-time Navy, white bell-bottomed trousers and white jumper, bound at the cuff and the lower edge in blue.

"I'm asking for a draft home", he said. "I'm not going to stay here if you've gone."

"I don't know where we're going to end up," I said, "but as long as we're both based at home we can meet somehow."

Ours was not a friendship to be ended by a casual draft.

So at noon on a day of broiling heat not long after mid-summer we went aboard *HMS Ravager*. Allowing Wrens to go to sea on naval vessels was a new policy. We were not crew, merely transit passengers, and the change had been introduced following the relative improvement in warship losses as the intensity of the war receded. *Ravager* was not fully operational, having no squadron on board, and we were given the squadron's cabins. It meant bunks again, and Rachel and I hurriedly paired off so that we could again ensure our beloved choice of top and bottom bunk.

For the first time since we went to the Drafting Depot the previous year, we had an opportunity to get to know the six telegraphists from Winchester. Our twenty four-hour turns of duty in Gib had hitherto made it very difficult for us to make friends with them.

Late in the afternoon we set sail, and our last glimpse of Gib was of the big white concrete rain catchments on the eastern slopes. Eastern, because once more we were heading down the Med, this time to pick up a convoy which we were to escort home. The sharp bows of the carrier cut through the green seas, and ahead of us on the bow wave rode three magnificent speckled dolphins. All down the Med in the evening light they kept their stations beneath the prow, until the light faded and we could see them no more.

We *rendez-vous*-ed with the convoy and passed west again through the Pillars of Hercules in darkness, so we never saw the Rock again. Next day we were out on the wide Atlantic, and there in the convoy beside us was our old friend *RMS Orion*. But this time, it was we who were the escort.

Chapter X

The Far East Challenge

HMS Ravager was an American-built escort carrier, one of the lend-lease 'Woolworth' carriers. In a light sea she bucked and plunged like a bronco, and in a medium sea she pitched till the water broke over her flight deck. Our Mess, a small and airless cabin below, smelling strongly of diesel oil, proved unsavoury to our queasy stomachs, and in spite of the captain's efforts to keep us safely occupied by supplying us with ludo and dominoes, we took to wandering about the decks and sniffing the clean sea air. And that is what we were doing when, in the middle of the Bay of Biscay, the 'action stations' bell went, and *Ravager* cleared the decks for action.

We stood stock still where we were while for fifteen or twenty seconds every Seaman in the carrier ran to his action station. Then there was silence. Every gun was manned, and every asdic set, every radar set, every H/F D/F set. Quietly we slipped to our action stations, the Sick Bay. In the event of trouble, we had been told, go to the Sick Bay and nurse the wounded. We could not be sent to our cabins, as they were below the water-tight doors, and if the ship had been holed, we should have risked being trapped.

The Sick Bay was right up in those plunging bows. Every time we cleared a wave the deck fell from under us like a lift going down fast, until we shuddered into the next wave.

The MO decided to begin first aid lectures, though it seemed a little late in the day, as the wounded, if there were any, might come in at any minute. We sat on the heaving deck while he told us how to staunch blood. We held our heaving stomachs, and reminded ourselves that Lord Nelson, too, was often seasick. But no wounded were brought in, and after a while the all clear went.

That evening we wandered into the chart room. There, in the middle of the Bay of Biscay, was one white pin, and clustered round it were eight black ones.

"Aha," we said knowingly, "the white pin is us, and the black pins are the rest of convoy!"

"No," said the navigation officer, "the white pin is the convoy, and the black pins are the U-boats."

We went back to our cabins and began refilling our greatcoat pockets with sea-soap, lavatory paper, pearl necklaces, etc. We had no shipwreck rations or anti-mosquito cream, as none had been issued for this trip. That night we reverted to the outward-bound practice, and slept in our bell-bottomed trousers.

Although we had left the Med in tropical kit, our voyage north soon took us into grey seas and scurrying clouds. Five days out, the ship's company went into blues, and we put away our tropical kit for the last time.

When there was no flying we played hockey with the crew on the flight deck, using a coil of rope as a ball. But when we neared Britain there were planes from other carriers using our flight deck, so we took a ringside seat and watched, heart in mouth, as the Swordfish and Sea Hurricanes, guided by the man with the ping-pong bats, came fluttering out of the sky and trailed their little hooks to catch in the wires strung across our deck.

Most of us were making up for sleep lost during our year in Gib. We were all tired out, and although the ship had some sort of entertainment or activity lined up every night, we did not often take part, tumbling into our bunks by about 8 p.m. every night. None of us looked the better for our year on the Rock. We were hollow-eyed. We had all lost weight, partly because we were too exhausted to eat. I had been losing a pound a week for the previous twenty weeks. And we all had minor wounds, scratches and spots that would not heal. More than anything in the world we wanted seven days leave, seven days without night duty, and a chance to sleep and sleep and sleep. Aeons away were the days when, bursting with the energy of our teens, we had danced eight-some reels at the training establishment.

On our seventh day out we sighted Ireland, and *HMS Ravager* left the convoy and headed north alone. In the early evening we entered the Clyde.

It is the custom for the crew of HM ships returning from foreign parts to fall in on deck as the ship enters harbour. If there is a Marine band on board, it plays. As we anchored off Greenock, there was a fine turn-out of Wrens and sailors. It was a pity that the effect was spoilt at the last minute by the two smallest telegraphists, who tore across the flight deck at the most solemn moment, shouting shrilly "Wait for me— hey, wait for me".

That night the customs officers came aboard. One by one we stepped up to their table and handed in our declarations. In front of me Rachel stood, her hands clasped anxiously together.

"This cigarette lighter", said the officer. "Is it new?"

"Oh yes," said Rachel, "it's for a present."

The customs officer looked fiercely up beneath his bushy brows.

"Girl Guide?" he said, and wrote 'used' on her declaration.

It was my turn.

"This silk," he said, "where did you buy it?"

"In Gib", I said. I was bringing eight yards of silk home to my mother.

"Oh, then it's Empire silk", he said, and wrote 'Emp' on the form. He looked at the entry and pursed his lips.

"Is it *real* silk?" he said.

"Oh yes", I said, rather hurt at this suggestion that I was bringing home some shoddy bit of rayon.

"You never can be sure", said the officer. He wrote 'art' between 'Emp' and 'silk', worked out the duty, and said the duty on Empire artificial silk was not worth paying.

When it came to our wines and spirits though, it was a different story. The policy seemed to be to let the men in with liquor and tobacco, and sock them on perfumes and silks, and to let us in with feminine goods and sock us on cigarettes and gin. A very nasty bill awaited me on the crate I was bringing for my father. There was no question of my paying it, as I had spent all my money in Gib. I told the customs officer I was sorry, but I had no money with which to pay the duty.

"In that case, you had better drink the gin tonight on board", he said.

As he obviously could not really mean that we should sit in our cabins drinking gin, I took this as permission to take it ashore. As nobody took any further interest in us or our luggage, this was not a problem.

A WRNS Boarding Officer next came out to the ship, and told us to report back to the Depot of the Command in which we had first enrolled. That meant that I should have to say goodbye to all the others, and alone drag my luggage the length of Britain down to Devonport. Shortly afterwards, this order was countermanded, and we were told to report to the station from which we were drafted abroad; but this order was also changed, and ultimately we were all told to go to Portsmouth. The next night we caught the troop train south.

London was under attack from rockets and flying bombs. We went to Waterloo for the Portsmouth train, and went for breakfast in the station restaurant. It was fairly full, we could not sit together, and were scattered at different tables. The noise outside was appalling, as if a fleet of London buses were about to drive in. Suddenly there was silence. Our fellow-breakfasters promptly vanished under the table, or got up and rushed from the room for no reason that we could fathom. Scattered about the restaurant, the twelve of us sat and looked at one another across the thick station china, feeling foolish, and apprehensive at a situation we did not understand.

The flying-bomb assault had not been publicized either in Gib or on board *Ravager*. We did not know that the noise meant a flying bomb was approaching, and that the silence was the engine cutting out to bring the bomb down. We did not understand that the time had come to take cover. But we were lucky. The explosion, when it came, did not bring the windows in on us.

The problem of moving our luggage about was immense. Thanks to its vast expansion, I now possessed four suitcases and a kit-bag, plus my piano-accordion (which accompanied me everywhere), a container of gramophone records, a crate of liquor and a bag of fruit. There were no porters, and to make a dump and move things in relays was impossible alone, because any unguarded luggage risked being stolen. Everything in Britain was in such short supply that I suppose it was always worth stealing a suitcase, for the sake of what might be inside it.

We had moved our multitude of cases and kit-bags across Glasgow and across London, and suddenly I felt I was too tired to cope any longer. Not only could I not cope with my kit-bag any longer (it was nearly as large as I was, and about the same weight) but I could not cope with anything at all any longer. More than anything in the world I wanted my father to come and take the whole weight of coping off my shoulders.

But I did not know where my family was. Since March, to preserve secrecy about the pre-D-Day build-up of troops in England, all air mail to Gib had been stopped. Anything known in Gib was known in Berlin a few hours later. The last letter I had had from home was written three months previously, and told me that my father was being released from the Army and the family had found a flat in London, to which they would be moving, but I had never received an address.

I went to a phone box and rang up an aunt who lived in London. She was fascinated to know I was home from abroad, and wanted to chat, but I cut her short with "Where's my father?"

He was in South Wales. I tried another shot. "Is Uncle there?" I said.

It seemed that my uncle was in Norfolk. I must have been lamentably overtired, because at that I nearly burst into tears. I asked where my mother was, learnt that she had not, after all, come to London because of the flying bombs, but was staying with another aunt in Hertford. And with that I rang off, having indulged in no happy chat and explained nothing to my aunt.

It seemed pointless to take the fruit and the silks and the accordion and all the rest to Portsmouth. We should be sent on disembarkation leave at once anyway, and I would pick it all up on my way back through London. I put it all in the left luggage office, and went on with hardly any luggage at all.

At Portsmouth there was some sort of confusion, and an attempt was made to draft us abroad. Patiently we explained that we were *from* abroad, and wanted leave.

We were told there was no such thing as leave — it had been cancelled indefinitely for all Forces since the D-Day landings.

We were tired of being ordered about, and were determined to go on leave. We were rather firm about it, and an hour or two later we were on our way back to Portsmouth station, with leave warrants in our pockets.

We had now been on the move for about thirty hours. We got into a Pullman coach, put our heads on the table and fell asleep. We were far too exhausted to remember that there had once been a time when a journey was a hilarious adventure shared with exuberant tars. Grey under our tan, our white shirts filthy and sweat-stained from travel and the exertion of luggage hauling, we slept fitfully all the way to London.

Here we split up in pairs to cope with the luggage. Jointly Sheila and I relayed her luggage by gentle stages to her home in Wimbledon. Then she returned to Waterloo and jointly we took mine to King's Cross so that I could join my mother in Hertford. I left most of it at Hertford station, but set off for my aunt's house carrying two suitcases. They proved too much for me, and half way there I just left the first one, and a little further the other, in the road. I was beyond caring whether they were stolen or not. I reached my aunt's house with nothing but what I stood up in, and knocked on the door. My blue uniform hung round me in folds from the weight I had lost since I went abroad, and I was almost too tired to stand.

The door opened. My mother and my aunt were there excited, welcoming.

"Here you are!"

"It's Anne! Anne's home!"

"Come on in! Tell us all about it!"

"Where's your luggage, darling?" said my mother.

"It's along the street somewhere", I said, and burst into tears. "Please, can I go to bed?"

Which is what I did. We spent our seven days' leave asleep. At the end of the week, we were woken by a telegram extending our leave for a further week. So it was a dozen fairly spry telegraphists who reported back to Portsmouth, and were sent on to Southsea to await draft.

At Southsea we were given six mattresses between the twelve of us, and told to sleep in the basement in a small room normally used as a broom-storage and cleaning room. As Portsmouth and Southsea were being attacked by rockets and flying bombs, the Admiral had given orders that no Wrens were to sleep above ground level.

The broom-cupboard was large enough to have a window, but there were already seven other Wrens and four mattresses in it, so it was quite a squash. Head to tail, without space to turn over, we slept there for the next week.

On the first day we reported anxiously to the Drafting Depot, but there was no word of a draft awaiting us. Instead we were told to go and scrub out the various Wren Quarters in Portsmouth and Southsea.

We were indignant. Scrubbing out other Wrens' quarters, we maintained, was no job for Leading Wrens. In the end our arguments prevailed, and we were assigned in couples to go and 'supervise scrubbing'.

Doris and I were detailed to go to the same address. Gloomily we left the Drafting Depot, and automatically our steps turned towards Portsmouth. After a while I said, "Do you know the way?"

"No," said Doris, "perhaps we'd better ask someone."

"Yes", I said. "What is the address we're supposed to find?"

"I don't know", said Doris. "I wasn't listening when she said. I thought you were."

"No," I said, "I thought you were."

We went for a cup of coffee while we thought about this. Six or eight of the others gravitated into the same café, and none of them knew where they were supposed to be.

We decided to go to the pictures.

The next day we went to the pictures again.

At the end of the week an angry Chief Wren burst into the fo'c's'le at our quarters and glared at us.

"You lot", she said. "Report to me in the morning."

We had been rumbled.

"Sorry, Chief", we said politely. "Can't. It's Sunday. Church parade."

"Very well. Monday morning."

The next day twelve pious faces appeared on Church Parade. Our piety was rewarded. That very night we were ordered to report on Monday morning to a training depot in London, where on arrival we were promoted from basement broom-cupboard to a window-less corridor on the second

floor lined with double bunks. The cabins on the upper
floors had been abandoned because of doodle-bug bombing.

Our task now was to switch our skills to the Far East, and
that meant learning Japanese Morse. Western Morse assigns
a Morse symbol to each vowel and consonant, each numeral,
and then there are a plethora of other symbols covering e.g.
punctuation. Japanese script is based on primary syllables,
not individual letters, thus each word is broken down not
into separate consonants and vowels but combinations of a
consonant accompanied by a vowel. The Japanese word for
ship, for instance, *maru*, takes four Morse symbols in the
West, but only two in Japanese, *ma* and *ru*. However, though
no symbols are required for vowels, the net effect is to
require far more symbols, as each consonant-plus-vowel
combination requires a fresh symbol. So where twenty-six
symbols sufficed for our alphabet, the Japanese needed
seventy-six apart from numerals, punctuation, etc.

Obviously, whatever we wrote down was going to bear
no resemblance to what a Japanese telegraphist would be
writing. Reading Western Morse was too deeply embedded
in our responses to be eradicated, so on hearing a digit we
continued to write what we'd always written—e.g. on
hearing 'dah-dah' we wrote 'M'. The problem of the deficit
in symbols was solved by using, so far as we could, what
were called 'barred letters', which were symbols incorpo-
rating the familiar Morse pattern, but with a distinguishing
extra bit. An 'L' for instance transmitted as 'dit-dah-dit-dit',
but an 'L-bar' transmitted as 'dit-dah-dit-dit-dah', and was
indicated in writing by drawing a line (a bar) over the letter.
We were accustomed to barred letters. A lot of the German
U-boat stations had incorporated them in their call-signs.
Using barred letters got us up to some sixty symbols, but it
still wasn't enough, so new symbol-scripts had been
devised, writing, for instance, a triangle, or an 'L' backwards.
The problem of translating all this written gibberish into
Japanese syllables (which would of course still be meaning-
less, as it would be in code) was for the code-breakers, not

us, to solve (at least for the moment, though that was later to change). Just as in the old days when we first learnt Morse, we now had to work up our speeds and master the Japanese 'operators' chat'.

Our instructors were 'Singapore Chiefs', girls who had gone out to Singapore in 1941 with one of the earliest over-seas drafts of WRNS telegraphists. They had escaped from Singapore three weeks before its Fall to the Japanese, and afterwards they had worked in Colombo. In the spring of 1942, when the Royal Navy had been pressed back towards Africa and Naval Far East headquarters had thought it prudent to leave Ceylon (Sri Lanka), they had moved again, this time to Kilindini in East Africa. Returning to England a year later, a number of them had been aboard the *Empress of Canada*, which was torpedoed off West Africa, and their collected treasures went to the bottom, but, unlike the first Gib telegraphists, they themselves had all survived.

We sat open-mouthed as they told us of lions and rhinos in Africa, of leave spent among the tea plantations in the hills of Ceylon, of Chinese dinner parties in Singapore. By the time they had finished, we were all on the verge of volunteering to go abroad again, but we restrained our-selves. With calculated prudence, we were not going to volunteer again unless we could get promoted, and so earn better living conditions. So far there was no word on that score, the Admiral's signal remained the only indication of our being Leading Wrens, but as we'd been either on draft or in transit almost since then, we were not too surprised.

Doodle-bug attack was proving disruptive. So frequent were the air-raid warnings that many institutions, including ours, ignored the general alarm, and only took cover when the 'yellow' alarm was changed to 'red', indicating that a bomb was actually approaching our vicinity. Muffled inside our headphones, we never knew when the red warning went. Our instructor would send us sharp red alert warn-ings in Morse on the buzzer, whereupon we would take pencil and signal pad, and, still wearing headphones, crawl under the table and continue our instruction. But after a week of this it was decided that there were too many bombs interrupting our work, and we were sent out of London.

Once more we packed our kit-bags and left, this time to return to Scarborough. Travelling with us were some Army girls from the gun sites on the East Coast. They fell asleep almost as soon as the train started. They were as tired as we had been when we returned from Gib. They were on duty alternate twenty-four hours, but the guns were blazing so constantly that in practice they were scarcely ever off, as when nominally off duty they had to stand by to relieve the duty watch when they became too exhausted to carry on. The flying bombs droned steadily over, day and night. Those girls were justifying their existence in those months as we felt we had done during the Battle of the Atlantic, two years previously.

Back in Scarborough we gazed around us in surprise. There was scarcely a soul we knew. All our contemporaries had gone. Some had married and started families, some had gone into other work, most had been drafted to Colombo. But Gay was there, still not yet twenty-one, but a Watch Petty Officer now, and an instructor.

She was changed. Eight months previously she had married a Canadian Air Force navigator. He had been recalled from their honeymoon, and within three weeks of their marriage his plane had failed to return from a raid over Germany. That was all she knew.

There were flocks and flocks of new little Wrens. They accorded us the sort of respect we had given Grannie, back in Devonport days. We felt old and wise; the first knell, perhaps, to mark the passing of our youth. When they heard we were veterans of overseas service, their envy and admiration soared to greater heights.

"Gosh," they sighed, "overseas! Simply heaps of men! You must have had fun!"

"Oh yes", we said evenly. "Yes. We had terrific fun."

"Were you *madly* gay*?"

"Yes." It was no use trying to explain. "Yes, we were madly gay."

They told us about the station. There was a new MO, and he was terribly handsome. Drafts of sailors had come … drafts of sailors had gone … Was it possible, we asked ourselves, that we had ever been so naïve, so spontaneous?

In the evenings they put on their best kiss-proof lipstick, and went dancing. We watched them go. We could barely afford to go to the cinema. All our papers were apparently missing, so we could not be paid as Leading Wrens — in fact, we could not even be paid as telegraphists. We were qualified only for the lowest unskilled pay rate until our papers could be traced with actual documentary proof that we were Leading Wrens and had been trained in a specialized category. One of our former officers sent us a message 'welcoming back the cream of the W/Ts', but we were unmoved by this soft soap, and it was Beryl who suggested that we reply that the cream had gone sour, though I don't think we actually did so.

We went back to work in the same isolated cottage (not needed since the construction of the modern underground station) that had housed the tiny fug-laden watch-room of our first hours on the job. By mid-September we had successfully taken the exams that concluded our Japanese course, an achievement that would have entitled us, had we officially existed, to 2d a day additional pay. We embarked immediately on the Petty Officers' course, and spent our evenings studying. The words 'atom' and 'hydrogen' had not yet acquired a sinister connotation, and we were learning that 'an atom is composed of a positive nucleus surrounded by one or more electrons, negative. A hydrogen atom has one electron, and a uranium atom has ninety two electrons to each nucleus.'

---

*   See p. 107.

The tablecloths in the Mess became covered with indentations where, with the ends of forks, we traced out the circuits of potentiometer and rheostat. Gently we were led from the study of magnetic fields to the electric bell and the telephone, inductance, transformers and condensers. We studied radio valves, diode valves, triode valves, tetrode valves, pentode valves (my schoolgirl Greek was finally coming in useful) and, at long last, the super-heterodyne receiver, with the final warning 'sometimes the detector, AVC and First Audio Valve is all included in a double diode triode'.

Examinations started. There were written papers and practical exams. An RN Lieutenant conducted the practical exam. He asked me various questions, and then said:

"Now, I want you to imagine that a Wren is operating a wireless set in a little hut in a wood. Along come two matelots, and they let the aerial down. What will happen?"

"Well," I began, "she'll lose her ..."

She would lose her signal, of course, but why *exactly*? I should know perfectly well, but a sudden exam panic had seized my mind, and I could think of nothing clearly at all. Obviously "Why?" would be the Lieutenant's next question, so I must stall for time on the first while I thought out the answer to the second.

"She would lose her ... er ... um ..." I said again.

To stop the wheels of my brain racing so uncontrollably, I slowly re-thought the situation. There was the hut, all by itself in the wood. There was the Wren all by herself in the hut. Creeping among the trees were the two matelots ... Now, the tricky bit about the aerial ...

"She would lose her ..." I looked up. The Lieutenant was pink in the face and staring at the floor.

"She would lose her signal", I said hurriedly.

He breathed out loudly, and did not ask me why. We left the subject of Wrens in lonely huts and went on to other topics.

Afterwards I heard that I got 100% in technical wireless. This was impressive, and a girl brought me her wireless set to mend. I took the back off and looked inside, but it did not seem to bear any relation to the diagrams I had so carefully learnt, so I put the back on again, shook it, thumped it suddenly on the back as for hiccoughs, and it went very well after that.

We were drafted again, this time back to the Signals School in Hampshire where we had first trained. Memories of the farm we had financed returned to us. We were to do a course in High Frequency Direction Finding, and we did not intend to be deflected by chickens or ponies, milking goats or mucking out pigs.

At some stage during our peregrinations, we had been present at a lecture from a WRNS officer, telling us that she was sure we were all going to be simply splendid, and the WRNS was just the grandest service. We did not want pep talks, we wanted our missing pay papers—we were still being paid at the minimum unskilled rates. And yet, all too often our officers seemed to believe that all that was necessary was to treat us like Sea Rangers enjoying a pro-longed game of playing at sailors. Indeed, at one stage during our travels, one of us, desperate over missing pay, went to the First Officer to ask for a pay advance, only to be told that 'no gel without private means should have got herself into the WRNS'. We were, with a vengeance, expected to be an elite.

The truth was we had become somewhat belligerent. Our stroppiness must have shown in our faces. When we arrived at the Signals School, Authority took one look at us and decided to split us up, one in each cabin. But the Mess committee was elected one from each cabin, and when the committee met, ten of us had got ourselves elected. We ran the Mess committee. There really was no need for us to be so belligerent, the management of the school had changed since we had been there before, and beyond terrorizing the galley and insisting that twelve girls needed twelve slices of bully beef, not ten, we had very little to do. Even so, we were followed round admiringly by several classes of new entries who said they had been hungry for weeks.

Gluttonous for work, as usual, we flung ourselves zestfully into our new course. Pen and pencil proved inadequate, and we acquired a battery of coloured crayons. The ozonosphere, the stratosphere, the ionosphere, the E and F layers went gaily onto paper in different colours. We learnt about types of direction-finding equipment, we wrote exam papers, and the RN Lieutenant returned and gave us a new practical examination. He removed vital parts of the set's interior, and when we each went separately into the examination room, he just told us to switch on, and left us to discover that the set would not work, and then to find out why.

We had often had trouble with sets which would not work, and a Wren called Mary (one of the Flowerdown six) had devised an excellent formula for putting them right. One went to the other side of the room, looked out of the window, and whistled. Then, very suddenly, one rushed back across the room and turned on all the necessary knobs, and quite often we caught the set off-guard, before it had had time to go contrary, and it would work very well. We doubted if this procedure would work with the Lieutenant.

We resorted to a rather mean device. When the Lieutenant went for his tea, the eight of us who had not yet been examined got into the exam room and, working as a team on the problem, found out what was wrong. All that we had to do after that was each in turn to go through a pantomime of pretended amazement when the set refused to function, and then make diligent search until we decided the moment had come to 'discover' what was wrong.

I don't think he was deceived. Two of the girls failed.

Before we became fully qualified as Petty Officers, we were sent back again to Scarborough, where we spent a week working watches in an isolated hut surrounded by courteous Italian prisoners-of-war tilling the fields of beet and cabbage. Then we went to Chelmsford, where, among more beets and cabbages, we put in another week of experience. At this point our horizons were enlarged by sessions at the Marconi Research station and at the Crompton Parkinson electro-engineering works, where we were fascinated to observe electrical equipment bearing Russian script, and destined, presumably, for the Arctic convoys making their perilous way through the U-boats and ice-bound seas to Murmansk. No one could know that this was to be the last winter of that ghastly experience.

Chelmsford brought us back into doodle-bug territory again. When they came noisily overhead, we used to switch off the wireless in the fo'c's'le so that we could hear if the engine cut out, indicating the bomb was descending, but mostly they went over us to London. This preyed on our imaginations; the thing was going to come down *somewhere*. In a way it was a relief when the sinister purring in the skies suddenly sputtered out, and we knew that one at least was *not* going on to obliterate our loved ones. Several of us had relatives in London—including me; my family had found a basement flat to rent and had re-assembled itself in Central London (not too expensive, as there wasn't much demand for flats in Central London at the time).

In the fo'c's'le the seconds that elapsed between the failure of an engine and the explosion were passed in a petrified stillness as if time had ceased. Those writing letters would sit looking at the last word written, pen poised without movement; those sewing and knitting paused in the middle of a stitch. We didn't look at one another. When the explosion came, we resumed our activities without comment exactly where we left off, like a film that had jammed and suddenly started again. If some of us were thinking of the crushed and mangled bodies that must be lying not very far away, we did not say so to one another.

At last we were considered fully trained. In London, all danger of invasion long since past, the Home Guard were holding their final parade before being disbanded. Large crowds were cheering them. If Hitler's paratroops had ever landed, those grandfathers of ours would have resisted to the last man, but now their task was done.

For us, there was still work to do. We were on our way to *HMS Flowerdown,* outside Winchester.

Chapter XI

Over and Out

Though far from the sea, we were once more back in a big naval establishment. We were divided up among the watches, Rachel and I being together, and we were joined by two of the former Winchester telegraphists who had been in Gib with us, Evelyn and Beryl.

Beryl had a lovely soprano voice, liquid and effortless. She had been soprano soloist in Gibraltar Cathedral when we sang *The Messiah*. Evelyn was half-Belgian, half-Irish; she spoke fluent French and Italian, and had a colleen's creamy complexion, blue eyes and dark hair. She had grown up on the Continent, and seemed to us the epitome of elegance and sophistication. Her home had been in Brussels, and when the Germans occupied Belgium, her home had become a German officers' Mess. During that autumn of 1944 the Nazi armies had been pushed out of Brussels, and Evelyn's family learnt that, with meticulous rectitude, the Germans had paid rent for the house into a Brussels bank, where it now awaited them. And they had not discovered the family valuables, which had been hurriedly buried under the tennis court.

As in Gib, the accommodation was a Nissen hut, but instead of beds the twelve occupants shared six double bunks. Among the other eight were two other telegraphists, Pam, a big cheerful girl with an encouraging way of addressing everyone vehemently as 'my dear old soul', who had trained with us originally, having come from the Argentine to join up; and a bubbly, blonde, newly-trained

telegraphist named Ricky. The other six were not telegraphists. One of them was shortly replaced by a girl we had
known in Gib, and she joined us as thin and ghostlike as we
had been when we first returned. She stayed in her bunk
sleeping all her free time, and we used to fetch her food over
from the Mess for her.

The winter was beautiful. Snow came, and frost; the sun
was red, and the sky grey and pink. White mist clung to the
trees and strands of frozen vapour hung in the air, as if some
monster had passed by and left a trail of crystallized breath.
Icicles two feet long dripped from the eaves of our hut, and
when we ran to the ablutions block to wash or bath, our
breath froze in a lacy white frill round our faces. We fought
our way through midnight snow storms into the bright
lights and warm air of the watch-room.

After the heat of our hut in Gib we felt the difference. The
fuel supply gave out, and we followed the naval stokers
about begging them to drop shovels of coke for us to
salvage. Finally, in desperation, we took a chair to pieces and
burnt it in the stove in our hut. I tried not to think about the
'Brutal and Licentious' Soldiery who had so shocked me by
reputedly burning the furniture in my old school.

We were back at work. Occasionally we worked on
German frequencies, more often on Japanese, and were soon
trusted with those that were most demanding. On the
German, it was noticeable that there had been a marked
deterioration in the quality of the German operators. Later it
was to be claimed that some seventy-five per cent of German
U-boat crews perished at sea, and by 1945, though there was
no falling off in the crispness of their operators' touch,
always good, they were less well trained than before. Often
we knew their operating procedures better than they did
themselves, and listened apprehensively to their mistakes,
anticipating the ticking-off they would get from their con-
trols, sometimes terminating in an apologetic piece of
'operators' chat' Q-code hitherto unknown to us, signifying
'junior operator on watch'. The level of hostile activity was

clearly slackening, indeed on April 22nd the black-out ended in London, and for us at work, as in Gib when the Italians surrendered, there was sometimes virtually nothing to do. By early May 1945 we were listening to messages transmitted un-coded, in German plain language, and it was clear the European war was about to end.

I was lucky enough to be on a special all-day stand-off on May 8th, VE Day. I headed for London. There was very little traffic on the roads, and I didn't risk hitch-hiking. Instead, together with a fellow Wren, I took the train to Waterloo. Plenty of people milled about in the streets, but there was little hilarity, and those in fancy hats looked rather self-conscious. By mid-afternoon Piccadilly was crowded, and we went on to Westminster to watch the procession of MPs attending a Thanksgiving Service in the Abbey. My walk home to call on my family took me up Whitehall, where the War Office was striving for exuberance, and was letting off coloured smoke bombs. I stayed at home to listen to the broadcast speeches by the King and allied commanders, then in the evening headed out to the Mall and Buckingham Palace, where happy crowds ceaselessly sang *Land of Hope and Glory* and called for the King. By now it was evening, and when the Royal Family appeared on the balcony the Queen was in a white evening dress with shining tiara, the King in naval uniform, Princess Elizabeth in her ATS uniform. Perhaps it was just after that that the two princesses made their now-famous escape into the crowd, for it was then that a Guards' band appeared, we fell in behind them, and marched with them to Wellington Barracks. Then home, via Whitehall, Trafalgar Square and Charing Cross Road. The huge crowds were happy, but very restrained, almost solemn. People seemed all too aware of those whose celebration was scarred by heart-break, and those whose people were still at peril in the Far East.

The Far East became the focus of our efforts. That spring there was a challenging innovation. It was realized that a whole stage of decoding Japanese messages could be simplified if the process of translating the Latinate letters we were writing into Japanese syllables could be eliminated. We could not write in Japanese, but the ingenious solution was devised of creating typewriters whose keyboards mirrored the (mostly Latin alphabet) symbols to which we were accustomed, but the actual key when struck typed the appropriate Japanese Morse equivalent. The drawback was that we were not typists. The US Navy trained its telegraphists as typists, but in 1942 when we joined up we were needed urgently on the job, there was no time to train us as typists, and any girl already skilled in typing was directed to the Writers' category, where her skills were needed, not retrained as a telegraphist. Also, it must be said, in the difficult conditions in which we, as interlopers, were often operating, it was a great help to have a hand free to manipulate knobs.

Initially, we had only two of the new typewriters. It was the Gibraltar Wrens who were given the task of pioneering the new response. We were competent, and we knew it. But pride was about to come before a fall. We were given twenty-four hours, i.e. a full round of watches, to familiarize ourselves with the new typewriters, and then became operational. I suppose there was an assumption that women could instinctively type (the conviction that women are born able — and destined — to type has proved deep and long-lasting). It was hectic and nerve-wrecking, and I do wonder how accurate we managed to be, but we only had to keep going for five hours at a time. The ten-hour afternoon-and-evening stint that, in Scarborough, had bought us a 'stand-off' every fourth day did not apply at Flowerdown, where, as in Gibraltar, it was split into two watches (1300–1800, 1800–2300). The long 'Middle' watch, from 11 p.m. to 8 a.m., was not too demanding, because the Far East always faded out at night (thanks to the influence of those 'Layers' we had studied so diligently on our course).

During May atmospheric changes began which, by mid-June, meant that the Far East was audible all night. One June night, after six and a half hours of non-stop reception, my pride collapsed and I called for a relief (a sailor with pencil and signal pad took over from me). I went outside into the fields that surrounded the watch-room, into a dewy, flower-filled dawn. After about twenty minutes I felt sufficiently in control of my nerves to return to the watch-room, where I found my Wren colleague with her head on her typewriter, sobbing. At 8 a.m. we warned the girls taking over from us for the Forenoon watch (who would be due back at the end of the day for the coming night's Middle watch), and they thanked us politely, but clearly thought us wimps. The next night they too both collapsed in tears. It was humiliating. We never escaped from the sense of needing to prove we could do a job as well as the boys, and now we'd given grounds for the boys to say the girls weren't up to it. But they were not put to the test. More typewriters were obtained, more girls given more time to train on them, and after that the night watch was split, and no one had to do more than five hours at a stretch operationally, which we managed to achieve.

Nobody knew how long the Far East War would go on. In February a notice had gone up asking anyone with a knowledge of Greek to come forward. I surmised that prob-ably people familiar with a non-Latinate script were being sought as a prelude to training in Japanese, and duly reported to our First Officer, who said the notice only applied to men. She wanted to know, though, how I had come to do Greek at school, and I explained to her about the place at Lady Margaret Hall which I had rejected in order to join up.

"You must go back", she said. "My old college! You *must* go back."

It was the first of a series of pressures that were brought to bear on me to choose Oxford as my post-war destination —if, that is, I could succeed in a second application, which was by no means a foregone conclusion. My old head-mistress wrote with the same advice, and my father was particularly keen that I should try again. My mother, meanwhile, was on a different tack. Why, she wanted to know, did I not after all this time apply for a commission? I explained that in the WRNS it just wasn't 'done' to apply for a commission, you waited to be recommended. Then why, she wanted to know, had I not been recommended? After all, I'd had a good education, been trusted with responsibility at school (head of house, senior prefect), respectable family ... *what had I been up to that made me ineligible?* I explained that much the same applied to all the other Tels (SO). In that case, she said, wasn't it about time my father spoke to ... "NO!" Pull strings to get a commission? Perish the thought! My lot was thrown in with the telegraphists, and there I was content it should stay. Besides, I explained, with typical Tel (SO) arrogance, it took a good six months to train one of us. You could train a new WRNS officer much more quickly, so we were more valuable where we were.

The problem of our delayed promotion was, however, a different matter. On our arrival at Flowerdown in early December 1944 our new Captain had won our hearts on interviewing us by remarking (unprompted) that something had clearly gone awry with our promotion. We were working under Petty Officers who had only been in training when we were already proceeding overseas. But the weeks went by and nothing changed. By the beginning of January '45 I had qualified for my three-year Good Conduct Badge, and had no hesitation in applying for it, now that I had the Leading Rate anchor on my arm to prove that the three years had not passed totally without achievement. It was slow to come through, but on April 4th the Captain saw me in a formal ceremony and awarded me my three-year G.C. badge. To my delight the fortnightly pay parade at the end of April yielded me £7, including a bonus for back pay since January for the stripe.

Neither stripes nor anchors exempted us from basic chores, however. Our Portsmouth contention that Leading Rates did not scrub cut no ice at Winchester, and as May advanced, and the German war ended, I found myself really resenting the fact that, well into my fourth year, I was still on my knees scrubbing lavatories like a new recruit. No amount of using naval terminology and calling them 'heads' really helped. I sat back on my heels and took a decision. Pulling strings was wrong in principle, but was it wrong if you only wanted what you had earned? I talked it over with the others. And wrote a letter.

We had gone behind our officers' backs. It was not because we distrusted them; on the contrary, at Winchester they were excellent officers, accessible, interested and, wherever their writ ran, effective. But it wasn't in their power to overcome the Nameless, Faceless power of the higher bureaucracy. On various dates in late May and early June those of the Gibraltar contingent who had passed the PO course were rated Petty Officers. We were given so much back seniority that we ranked with the first promotions of our branch. It took time — but in mid-July my fortnightly pay totalled the munificent sum of £36 10s, including back pay. So we learnt that the world can be made to pay 20s in the £ after all — provided, that is, that one knows the right people. Again a knell sounded for innocence lost. And nothing could buy back for us those walks into Spain that had eluded us because of our lowly rank.

We had been well trained. We were not afraid of work or of responsibility. Without qualms or difficulties we took over as watch Petty Officers. We cut the black buttons from our jackets and sewed on brass. Crossed anchors went on our sleeves instead of the single 'killick' above our three-year badges. We discarded our sailor caps and wore tricornes. We moved to better cabins, two to a room with beds not bunks, and ate in the POs Mess. But nobody suggested a celebration party.

Meanwhile I'd been in touch with Lady Margaret Hall, and been invited to an interview on a date three days after the PO rating came through. The A34 ran straight from Winchester to Oxford, so following my normal travel arrangements I went out onto it, and almost immediately got a lift from two sergeants in an Army truck. We reached Oxford rapidly, and they kindly toured the city till we found Lady Margaret Hall. It proved to be a red brick building much the colour of my old school. I was not due there until the afternoon, so, having found it, I went back to the centre of the town, and repaired to the Randolph Hotel for coffee. It was very slow to arrive. Finally, a young man impeccably dressed in civilian clothes approached me.

"Excuse me, Madam", he enquired. "Are you an officer?"

"No," I replied, resplendent in my recently-acquired brass buttons, "I'm a Petty Officer."

"Then I'm sorry," he said, "but I'm afraid I must ask you to leave. We do not serve Other Ranks."

So, after all that effort, I had not 'arrived' after all. I left, and went along the road to the Cadena café, where I got lunch.

Back at LMH the corridors seemed to be swarming with plump little girls in blazers saying "Golly!" I read the notice board in the hall, from which I got the impression that special permission must be obtained to attend mixed parties, or stay out after 10.30 p.m. I felt very very old indeed.

There were interviews. My original application had been to read English, but now the metaphysical poets seemed aeons away. Was there not something more practical that I could do? It was decided that I should apply for a place to read Philosophy, Politics and Economics. I left armed with a book list so that I could do some relevant reading.

I started work on a book on Logic. I had to re-read each sentence several times to understand it, and when I did understand it, I was monumentally unmoved. I abandoned logic for the moment, and started on the historical biographies.

Duncan had got back to the UK early in 1945. We had been separated for six months, and had the chance to think about the folly of a friendship doomed by chasms of incompatibility in our backgrounds, in religion, education and class. I'd taken him home, and everyone did their best, but the atmosphere was stilted at best. We agreed to part. I drenched a naval signals pad in tears, and he failed his exams. Then, quite unexpectedly, we met on the escalator at Waterloo station, and decided that Fate had intervened to keep us together. He was stationed only about twenty miles away, so through the green English spring and summer we met when our off-duty days coincided, and wandered through the Hampshire countryside, making friends with the squirrels and rabbits, stopping for beer and sandwiches in Red Lions and White Harts. We did not talk about the future.

Towards the end of June, I got a letter from Oxford offering me a place, to be taken up in October if I could get released, otherwise for the following January. On the very same day, Wrens with either degrees or Higher Certificates were asked to volunteer for a course in Japanese language, prior to a draft abroad for a maximum of two and a half years. My feet still itched to travel. Perhaps even now I could see the Taj Mahal and Kandy, pick wild orchids in Malaya or smell the spicy breezes of the Indies.

But there would not be a third chance for Oxford. Even the second was a bit of a miracle. Numbers of women permitted at Oxford were tightly controlled, but permission had been given for six places to be added to the LMH quota for the year 1945-6, provided they went to ex-Service women. The question was: what prospect was there of getting released to take up the place? Already a scheme had been announced for Class B demobilization for those returning to or taking up university places, but when I asked my First Officer's advice on this I learnt that it did not apply to women. I gritted my teeth, and let the chance to apply for the Japanese course go. In fact the war was to end so soon after, that I doubt if the course ever went ahead.

I wrote to Duncan and told him about the Oxford offer. He wrote back and congratulated me. And then he said that with this opportunity I should be moving into a world which was completely outside his reach. The words of the

captain at the RAF dinner in Gib came back to me ...
"someone who can give you what you'll miss if you don't go
to Oxford ..." I knew it was true. I wrote him my farewell. In
time the Future would seem far more important than the
Past. In time.

On August 7th I was sitting in a train on my way to Wales
on leave. Opposite me a man was reading his paper. He
opened it, and the front-page headline faced me: ATOMIC
BOMB DROPPED.

Gooseflesh came out on my arms. It spread to my legs
and prickled under my black stockings. Fear — not a
tumbled, panicky fear like my dread of poison gas, but a
still, vast, numbing fear — gripped me. Even the realization
that I was afraid frightened me, for it was our side that had
dropped the bomb, so why should I be so afraid?

Looking back, I know that I was frightened because at
that moment a philosophy of life collapsed and left me
shivering. Until that moment evolution and progress had, to
me, been two sides of the same coin. I had a boundless faith
in Humanity, and in Man as captain of his own destiny. But
at that moment it seemed to me that from now on Man was
to be the pawn, not the player; the pawn of a force so powerful, so far beyond the span of our imaginations that hence-
forth we would not control it, it would control us, and we
should be ants for the Furies to step on. When I had been
panicked by the thought of poison gas, I had turned to
Knowledge to drive out Fear. But this was a different Fear.
Knowledge could not control it.

I pulled myself together. Our side had dropped the
bomb. The war was almost over. The prisoners in the Far
East would come home at last, prisoners who had been out
there since before our 'Singapore Chiefs' fled to Colombo.
No more fine ships would go to the bottom, no more of the
sailors that I loved would die.

The Navy would not want us any more. It would not
matter to anyone whether we knew how a super-het worked
or not. Thirty words per minute or twenty, it would all be

the same in a month or two. For the last time we should work the Forenoon, the First and Middle watches. We should never again hear the naval prayer read — for the Fleet would no longer be 'the Fleet in which we serve'.

For a year or two, perhaps, we should reminisce about the days when we served with the Royal Navy. Later on, rather firmly, we should not reminisce, because we should not want people to know that we were old enough to have been in the Forces during the war.

There would be medals. When the invitations said 'Decorations will be worn', Wrens would polish up their husband's miniatures. Our own we would leave in cotton-wool at the back of the stocking drawer, or in the box with the collection of foreign coins.

High heels! I should have to learn how to walk in high heels! Most girls got through the tottering stage at the age of about sixteen, and I should have to face it at twenty-two. How humiliating. And civilian clothes ... how could one ever get out of bed in the morning if one had to decide what to put on?

There would be no rules about nail polish. I decided to buy the most vulgar and ostentatious colour I could find. Deep purplish-maroon would be nice, like the skin of a Victoria plum.

From the atomic bomb to plum-coloured nail polish in five easy minutes.

A week later the Japanese surrender was announced. I was in Porthcawl at the time, and we all went to the seafront, gathered round a bus shelter, and sang *Cwm Rhondda* (with harmonization) as frequently and as fervently as, in the Mall on VE Day, we had sung *Land of Hope and Glory*.

Work was diminishing. It began to feel somewhat as Gib had felt after the Italian surrender. But for many months we had been occupied with a series of lectures designed to return us to civilian life as responsible, well-informed citizens. We had lectures on the Commonwealth, Parliament and the BBC, and discussion groups on juvenile delinquency, freedom, nationalization, housing, equal pay and the economics of a declining population—a miniature PPE course in fact. We went to the local assizes, and were told to go to the Criminal Court, not the Divorce Court, as the Divorce Court was sordid. In the Criminal Court a sailor was being charged with the rape of a Wren. The defence was that the Wren asked for everything she got, and a number of ATS girls, also being processed into responsible citizens, looked at us in a rather nasty way. The next day's trainee citizens got a buggery case.

A draft of six Wrens was consigned to my care for a course at Southampton University on 'Government and the Citizen'. We met the mayor, saw round the civic centre, and were given a great deal of information about politics by two socialist lecturers who were determined to make good socialists of us all. They were typical of ABCA, the Army Bureau of Current Affairs, who were responsible for organizing the education that would propel us into the future as well-informed citizens, and who seemed to a man to be either dogmatic Marxists, or at least warm-hearted do-gooders with a total faith in the State to be both benevolent and competent. They put their opinions to us as if the opinions were facts, and we should probably not have noticed this if it had not been for a Leading Wren (not known to us, she came from a different naval establishment) who seemed to know just as many facts, but put quite a different interpretation on them. She turned out to be a PPE graduate from Lady Margaret Hall. Food for thought.

There was a WAAF officer on the course who admired the Chinese because, she said, they were inefficient. Efficient people were intolerant—look at the Germans. I was inclined to come down on the side of a little efficiency, myself, remembering the months of lost pay records and the chilling sense of non-existence. At that very moment, Naval Accounts were taking a final glorious swipe at me by deducting all the travelling expenses for the Wrens under my command from my personal pay. This led to a correspondence which did not end until after I had been demobilized, when I finally received the missing pay, and a letter that ended 'Your Obedient Servant, squiggle squiggle, Lt. Commander, for Director of Naval Accounts', which gave me some pleasure.

It was now late September, and we were devoid of useful occupation. Our officers gave a magnificent party for us, with turkeys, lobsters, oysters, trifles, cream cakes and cider cup. Half the Wrens were sent on what was called Accommodation Leave, but it was work we were short of, not space, and it was really Redundancy Leave. Rachel and Evelyn went, and we knew that when we next met it would not be as Wrens. By the end of September, I was the sole Petty Officer left on our watch, and next day I was told that I too was to depart on Accommodation Leave.

My efforts to get demobilized for college had come to nothing, but since we were all being dispensed with, it meant I could be at Oxford for the start of term, and I duly reported, and started work. Of course I had no civilian clothes or ration book, and I was still being paid as a PO Wren, but it was still a shock when, about ten days after the start of term, I was recalled to Flowerdown. I returned reluctantly, hoping my First Officer would prove under-standing, but she was away on leave, and her deputy reproached me severely for my conduct, pointing out I was still in the Navy. On my tearful plea that I had an essay on Gladstone to finish, she wrote me a railway warrant for Oxford, so for once I journeyed by conventional transport. A week later I was again recalled to Flowerdown, where the terminal medical inspections were conducted. Then with several others of our original draft we were despatched by naval transport to Portsmouth Barracks. We handed in our gas masks and our tin hats, and all but the clothes we stood up in. Four marines, also just demobilized, joined us on the train to London, and we threw a last wild, hilarious party, like the old days in the West Country, when we used to travel around Devon to Warship Week parades.

And then it was all over. Gay joined her husband on the Canadian prairies. He had survived the downing of his plane and been imprisoned in the notorious Stalag Luft III, though it was many months before the news of his survival reached her, and there was further hazard to come when the prisoners were force-marched west in atrocious winter conditions ahead of the advancing Soviet troops. Pam went home to the life of the English Club in Buenos Aires. Ricky got a job looking after a deputy governor's children somewhere along the upper reaches of the Nile. Rachel married an officer in a Sikh regiment, and went to Lucknow in time to see the sunset of the British Raj. Evelyn went home to Brussels, dug up her valuables from under the tennis court, and was soon in the sort of sophisticated and well-paid job for which her elegance and intelligence so well fitted her. Joy went to hospital, to battle for years against the debilitation she brought back from her service in the Far East, the same amoebic dysentery that my father had contracted in Gallipoli, whose life-long effects had condemned him to desk jobs when he rejoined his old regiment in 1939. I sold my piano accordion, had thicker lenses put in my glasses, and went back to Oxford.

Epilogue

Radio technology was to change swiftly and radically after World War II. In 1947 came the invention of the transistor, and much of what we had studied so diligently in our technical wireless classes became obsolete. Ahead lay the chip, the microchip, the computer, satellites and the NASA space programme with all the radical technological spin-offs that were to transform communications. By 1987 automated global satellite technology was replacing wireless telegraphy, and in the summer of 1997, half a century after our demobilization, the Royal Navy ended all training in wireless telegraphy (though Morse itself continued to have relevance for visual signalling). Before the Millennium ended, on February 1st 1999, Morse code had been officially superseded as a method of formal communication at sea.

Shortly before this, in 1993, the WRNS itself ceased to exist as a distinct entity, being incorporated into the Royal Navy with Wrens serving alongside sailors on equal terms bar (at the time) some restrictions applying to submarine service and the Royal Marine Commandos. The calling to which we had dedicated ourselves, and the Service within which that calling had been pursued, were no more. We had passed into History.

Glossary

ATS	Auxillary Territorial Service
CO	Commanding Officer
CPO	Chief Petty Officer
Fo'c's'le	Short for Forecastle: the forward part of a ship below the deck, traditionally used as the crew's living quarters.
GC	George Cross
GCHQ	Government Communication Head Quarters
H/F D/F Set	High Frequency Direction Finding
HRO	A US shortwave receiver
L/W	Leading Wren
MO	Medical Officer
NAAFI	Navy, Army and Airforce Institute
NCO	Non-commissioned Officer
OR	Other rank
PO	Petty Officer
POW	Prisoner of War
PX	General Store on US bases
QARNNS	Queen Alexandra's Royal Naval Nursing Service
RASC	Royal Army Service Corps
Rating	Seaman (non-officer)

RNVR	Royal Naval Volunteer Reserve
SO	Special Operator
VAD	Voluntary Aid Detachment (unit providing field nursing services)
VD	Venereal Disease
VE	Victory in Europe
VJ	Victory in Japan
WAAF	Women's Auxillary Airforce
WPM	Words per minute
W/T	Wireless Telegraphy
WRNS	Women's Royal Naval Service